Glasgwfield

Hartisfield

Garn[...]

C000217275

owcaldanes Burn

Glasgw

Colle[...]

Parsons Croft

Vicars Yairds

Beilcroft

Subchanters Croft

Easter

Wester Craigs

Provansyde Lands

Doghillok

Port

Stablegreen

North Metropolitan Port Church Yaird

Castle

Craiga Yett Port

St Nicholas Hospital

Quadrivium or Wyndeheid

Subdeans Mills

Ladywell

Crubbis Croft

Deynesyde

amshorne Lands

Well

Port

Port

Saint Ann's Croft

East Brig

Lang Croft

Flesh Market

Hutchesones Hospitall

Stinkand Vennd[...]

College and Yard

Blakfriars Kirk Cemetery and Yard

Old Vennel

Dowhill

Burn called Poldrait

The Butts

Muir

Carn[...]

Ove

Old Wynd or Vennel

Trongate

reet Cross

Midland Croft

New Wynd or Vennel

Nether

South Port

Gowgait

Vennel

Little St Kentigerns Kirk and Yaird

Ean Port

Round Croft

Egliscemeis Croft

Willia Aiker

Cropnestock Croft

Gallow

Witch Lone

Skinners Green

Linnings Haugh

Crooks

or

Kinclaith

Midam

Bramelands

Blackfauld

Burn

Camlachtie Burn

Burrowfield

Dalm[...]

OF ford

CLYD

Peitboa

Point Isle

d Brigend

nians Croft

Burn

Bird

uld

Little

Govan

Provosthaugh

OFFICE C

RESCUE HIS BUSINESS,
THE CLYDE HIS LIFE:

RESCUE HIS BUSINESS, THE CLYDE HIS LIFE:
The Story of Ben Parsonage & The Glasgow Humane Society

by
George Parsonage

GLASGOW CITY
LIBRARIES

Glasgow Humane Society,
Glasgow Green,
Glasgow G40 1BA.

ISBN 0 906169 29 1

Published By
Glasgow City Libraries Publications Board,
The Mitchell Library,
North Street,
Glasgow G3 7DN.
1990

Printed by
Cordfall Limited,
26 Civic Street,
Glasgow G4 9RH.

To Mother and Father

Ben Parsonage gave people a second chance at life, rescuing them from the murky waters of the Clyde. A rescue was his greatest reward in a lifetime of patrolling the reaches of the River. He was a small man, only 5'1" in height but he cast a giant shadow. He patrolled his beloved beat a shy unassuming boatman who single-handedly rescued more people from drowning than any man in Britain.

Terry Houston, *Daily Record*,
October 2nd 1979.

Contents

The Glasgow Humane Society

In 1787 a Glasgow merchant, James Coulter, left a sum of £200 in the care of the Faculty of Surgeons of Glasgow to set up a society for the rescue and recovery of drowning persons.

Before this time anyone attempting to take his own life was regarded as a criminal and seldom would anyone attempt to rescue you. Humane Societies were being set up all over the world, in New York, Paris, Milan, London. The Societies gave medals, certificates and money to anyone who assisted in the rescue or recovery of persons who had entered the water.

So it was that at a time when the French Revolution was taking place, and when Robert Burns was writing his poetry, a meeting was held in the Tontine Hotel, Glasgow, in August 1790 and the Glasgow Humane Society was born. Ten years before it had a Police Force, 34 years before there was a Royal National Lifeboat Institution, and more than 100 years before there was a Royal Life Saving Society, Glasgow had its Humane Society. While other societies (as did the London – now the Royal) became dedicated solely to giving medals and certificates, Glasgow appointed a full-time Officer and it became a very effective rescue service. As far as can be ascertained, Glasgow has the only working Humane Society still in existence.

In 1795 permission was given to build a boathouse and house on Glasgow Green. They were opened in 1796 and appear on the map of Glasgow of 1797. Between 1790 and 1857 no records of the Society's work have been found and it is unlikely that during this period there was an Officer. These were years of encouraging people by word of mouth, payment and the giving of medals for assisting those in danger of drowning.

A report of 1825 claimed that since the establishment of the Society the lives of 611 persons had been saved under the auspices of the Society. It is known that between 1790 and 1795 sets of apparatus were kept in the wash-house on Glasgow Green, and from 1795 to 1857 they were kept in the house which also served the role of a Receiving House.

During these years many ferrymen and others working on the river regularly received money from the Society for removing dead bodies from the water. John MacLean, Duncan Downie, James Geddes and John Geddes were some of these.

In 1826 the River Clyde was deepened to give 13 feet of high water at the

Broomielaw. Previously high water seldom reached what we now know as the Upper Harbour. In 1828 an increase is reported in accidents due to the extended and crowded harbour, the daily increasing travel by Steam Navigation and the prevailing practice of bathing which our dense population renders necessary and to which our fine River invites.

Between 1845 and 1859 there are records of many drownings and rescues of persons swimming in the river. During this period bodies were kept overnight at the Society House but in 1861 it was stated by the Humane Society Chairman that an arrangement had been made with the Police Committee by which all dead taken from the river should be immediately removed by Police Officers from the Society House.

The Directors take this opportunity of informing the Public that 9 lifebuoys have been placed by the Society at the following stations, 1 above the suspension bridge, 1 at the corner of the Fleshers Haugh, and 1 on the opposite side at Little Govan, 2 on the north and 1 on the south side of the river at the Dominie's Hole. 1 on both sides of the river at the Physic's Well above Rutherglen Bridge and 1 at the reservoir of the old water works, but they regret to add that from their necessarily exposed situations they are at considerable yearly expense in renewing or repairing the buoys and attached lines from the reckless and inconsiderate conduct of evil disposed persons whom it is the duty of the public to get discovered and punished.

Nowadays the lifebelts are looked after by Strathclyde Regional Council. Unfortunately they are still vandalised and the Officer retrieves an average of 150 belts and 70 ropes each year. The missing ropes are stolen to be used for many purposes.

Also in 1857 sums of 5 shillings, 7 shillings and 6 pence, and 10 shillings are recorded as being awarded for rescues.

In 1860 the *North British Daily Mail* carried the following extract from Society minutes *'The safety of the public would be promoted if a paling were erected along the edge of this part of the Canal.'* and in 1861 the *Glasgow Herald* quoted *'the alarming frequency of accidents and the fatal issue in which they so often result, demand that the matter should receive the immediate attention of the directors of the Humane Society, the authorities, or both, so that parties may be warned against bathing in such dangerous quarters [the River Clyde]'.*

Into this expanding city and river a full-time Humane Society Officer was introduced.

GEORGE GEDDES, OFFICER,
GLASGOW HUMANE SOCIETY, 1859-1889

In 1865 it is recorded that the Officer gave evidence before a Parliamentary committee concerning the effect that the removal of the weir would have – '*were the weir to be removed the stream would flow faster and in the case of heavy spates serious injury would be done to the river banks which moreover at low tide would present a disagreeable appearance and prevent people from walking by the Riverside'*.

In 1867 the Society House was extended and proper living quarters installed. In these years many persons are mentioned as helping the Officer, and when there was ice on the river two police officers were sent full-time to assist.

In 1871 the following sets of apparatus were kept – 1 set at the Broomielaw, 1 set at Finnieston. Each set contained 5 drags, 3 handcarts for carrying the body to a Receiving House in a proper posture, 3 mattresses (one for each hand cart), 12 pairs of blankets, 12 hand towels and 3 syringes. It is interesting to note that at this period bellows were used as an early form of artificial respiration.

In 1875 the Society minutes were quoted in the *Glasgow Herald*: 'the railing which, through the Society's efforts had been erected on the south side of the River, and extending from Wellington Street to Dixons property near Jennie's Burn has proved an invaluable safeguard as no accident has there occurred since its erection'. By 1988 this part of the river was again in need of a decent fence.

In 1878 it was the fatalities from bathing at the old springboards in the Clyde near the location of the present Corporation Boating Club Houses that caused the first public baths in Glasgow to be built at Greenhead and opened in 1878. From that time there was a decided fall in the recorded immersions in the area of Glasgow Green.

In 1877 George Geddes II, (the son) was awarded the Glasgow Humane Society Honourable Certificate.

In 1878/79 the weir at Glasgow Green was removed. Among other things this proved to be a danger to Rutherglen Bridge and it was closed in 1890. In 1880 life-hooks were placed all along the river banks.

GEORGE GEDDES II, OFFICER,
GLASGOW HUMANE SOCIETY, 1889 –1932

The records of the Geddes family contain accounts of all rescues and recoveries in the Glasgow area and further afield whether or not the Officer was involved, and therefore there is no way of acknowledging the rescues and recoveries the family undertook.

A newspaper of 1917 attributes George Geddes II with the rescue of 56 persons and his son Geddes George Junior with 10.

The river was very shallow in the days before the present weir was built and at low tide many bodies were seen lying on the sandbanks. These bodies were taken to the Mortsafe house or the District Receiving House, for example, the Gorbals Dead House, usually by hand cart. If not claimed they were taken away by the Parochial Board for interment. In 1900 George Geddes II and a crew of two were awarded a gold medal and a bronze figure at a lifesaving competition at the Paris Exhibition, and in 1901 George Geddes II was awarded the Silver Medal of the Royal Humane Society.

1904 – the first mention of a funeral van.

1911 – the first record of searches in the harbour area being undertaken on a regular basis.

1912 – the first mention of a motorboat.

1917 – George Geddes Junior awarded the Diploma of the Royal Humane Society.

1919 – Ben Parsonage's first recorded rescue.

Many of the boathouses that existed at this time and in the later part of the 19th century have now disappeared: Clutha, Rankines, Carrolls, Ures, McNeills, McGruers, Reillies, McWhirter's Aquatic Saloon, Working Men's Club and Tolbooth Lads.

Many ships were built on the Clyde during this time and the Officer must have witnessed famous ships such as the steamer *Killarney*, the bark *Marrion*, the brig *Kathleen*, the *Black Prince*, the Eagle steamers and the sailing herring boats come up and down the river.

In 1928 George Geddes Junior was drowned while attempting to save a man who jumped from the St Andrew's suspension bridge on Glasgow Green.

BEN PARSONAGE, OFFICER,
GLASGOW HUMANE SOCIETY, 1928 – 1979

In 1928 Benjamin Parsonage was appointed Officer in conjunction with George Geddes II.

1930 – Ben Parsonage awarded bravery award from Anchor Line.

1932 – George Geddes II died.

1936 – Ben Parsonage awarded Glasgow Corporation Bravery Medal.

1953 – Ben Parsonage awarded Bar to the Glasgow Bravery Medal.

1955 – Ben Parsonage awarded 2nd bar to the Glasgow Bravery Medal

1971 – Ben Parsonage awarded the British Empire Medal.

1971 – George Parsonage awarded Ben Parsonage, officer, Glasgow Humane Society 1928-1979 Glasgow Corporation Bravery Medal.

1971 – George Parsonage awarded Honourable Testimonial of the Royal Humane Society on parchment combined with resuscitation certificate.

1978 – George Parsonage awarded Strathclyde Regional Medal and Bar.

1978 – George Parsonage awarded the Mountbatten Medal of the Royal Lifesaving Society.

During the Officership of Ben Parsonage the Society was for many reasons able to become the unparalleled rescue service that it is today.

With the telephone, motorboats, police radios and boats on trailers able to rush to any locus in a matter of minutes, quarries, canals, ponds, lochs, indeed any waterhole became within easy reach of the Officer and many county police forces called on his services not just to rescue and recover bodies, but for the recovery of stolen goods.

Ben Parsonage was the longest-serving Officer of the Society and was responsible for saving at least 1,000 lives. The exact number will never be known as he was often so busy that there was no time to keep records. He was responsible for preventing thousands of accidents and recovering at least 1,000 bodies and an unknown amount of stolen property and weapons.

GEORGE PARSONAGE, OFFICER,
GLASGOW HUMANE SOCIETY, 1979 –

In 1979 Ben Parsonage died and was succeeded as Officer by his son George. Already in George's 10 years of service a great number owe their life to the readiness of the Officer and those aims of the Society laid out 200 years ago, and still practiced today.

1983, George Parsonage awarded Honorary Testimonial of the Royal Humane Society on Parchment.

1986, Sarah Parsonage (wife of Ben) awarded Chief Constable's Commendation.

Each of the Officers has had to deal with problems peculiar to their own decades, but one would be amazed at the amount and variety of work undertaken by the society. Although the list of Directors seems powerful, the Society has never been in a very healthy position financially. The Society maintains its independence, it is neither Regional nor District, it is neither police nor purely civilian, it has a foot in every camp, it is open to any member of the public to call upon its services, that way it can be of most use to humanity.

The Glasgow Humane Society has been fortunate during most of this century in having Officers from the Parsonage family who have been willing to spend their little free time building life boats and sheds, barges and oars, repairing wharfage, and fortunate also in receiving gifts of equipment from kind organisations and individuals. However, the Society premises now need to be renovated. It is to be hoped that by 1990, the Glasgow Humane Society's 200th anniversary, a renewal programme will be well under way if not completed. Much maintenance is required to keep a constant rescue service available. It is only if one is prepared both physically, mentally and has the necessary equipment to hand, that prompt action can be taken. Glasgow Humane Society's facilities centre around the Society House on Glasgow Green where until recently one room was kept as a mini-hospital for the attention of persons brought alive from the water. The speed of the Ambulance Service has more or less removed this need, but there is still part of the house, albeit on a lesser scale, set aside for such an emergency. The house is open for statements to be taken, for relatives of missing persons who need comfort, for persons who have thought of suicide but come to the house instead seeking comfort, and for the treatment of persons injured in the park, or on or near the river.

In the house, of course, is the telephone which is the hub of most emergencies, and everyone in the house plays a vital part. In the garden of the house sit two boats on trailers ready to be towed to any trouble spot. Two, because one never knows when a simple thing like a puncture might happen, or a serious problem,

16

like an accident occurring in the east of the city when one of the trailers was in the west. All eventualities have to be thought of. Each life boat contains 3 sets of oars in case, while rowing double-scull to a rescue, one might break.

At the riverside are two sheds on either side of a timber wharf. A gangway leads from the wharf to a timber barge, a step down to smaller, lower timber pontoons giving easier access to the boats moored alongside. There are different types of boats for different jobs. The rowing boat has been used more often than the motor boat for rescue, for many reasons it is more suitable, and the rowing boat is nearly always used for dragging operations. Therefore, two rowing boats are kept at the barges for rescue/dragging operations. These approximately 14 foot 6 inch-long boats are the fastest and lightest type possible while still allowing an 18-stone person to be lifted over the side.

For the occasion when fast travel further afield is required, or when items large or heavy have to be transported, motor boats are used – for example for the recovery of floating bodies, recovery of lifebelts, stolen goods, removal of rafts or raft material – and on occasions rescues quite far afield have been accomplished. Again, of course, there are two motorboats to allow for repairs, cleaning, and servicing, etc. Sometimes we are notified of an occurrence where the fastest means of giving help is to row to the weir, carry the boat round it and continue downstream; for this purpose a 10-foot light, fibreglass dinghy is kept in readiness. Again, of course, there is a spare. On occasions an accident occurs under a harbour wall where to achieve a rescue or recovery a boat has to be able to go between the quay wall piles, a light narrow boat is kept for this purpose.

Different types of engine are used. The launches use 40 h.p. engines, the trailer boats for long-distance work, for example, as far away as Erskine, have outboards available from 15 h.p. down to 1 h.p.

Between 10 and 12 boats are in readiness at any one time.

There are two sheds – one for repair and building work and one for storing materials, such as wood for small pontoons which require renewal every two or three years, planking, timbers, flooring, and wood for many other purposes, marker buoys, petrol, turps, emulsifying agents, paint, ladders and equipment like a boiler for steaming wood. There are many varied tools used for building and repairing boats and oar making; ropes of various types – for example wire and nylon, polypropylene, hemp; boathooks, poledrags, ropedrag, medical equipment, a stretcher, a resuscitator, protective and waterproof clothing of all types, rubber gloves, plastic sheets, hypothermia sheets, body-bags, etc.

Between the two sheds at present there is room for one boat to be repaired, painted or built at a time. The majority of boats in use for Society work are only lifted from the water during floods or for cleaning and painting and laid on the banking. Obviously we are open to the elements. No building has ever been sound enough to be heated, which would be a great help in drying out boats and for painting and varnishing them. A conglomeration of objects brought from the

river and awaiting destruction or collection is always stored around the premises
– oil drums, plastic drums, beer kegs, gas cylinders, road signs and cones, tree
stakes, lifebelts, rafts, raft material and many other items. It would certainly be
more pleasant if these could be stored out of sight.

200 years ago £200 started the Glasgow Humane Society, and since then
several thousand lives have been saved directly through its services and many
more indirectly. Many rended hearts have been put at ease by the recovery of the
bodies of their loved ones, and many lesser and varied problems have been
solved.

The ideals of Coulter and the Officers from the Geddes and Parsonage families
deserve to be continued in a manner befitting such a senior organisation.

A rescue station could be a suitable memorial to those people and credit to
the City of Glasgow.

The Society belongs to everyone, it is for the use of all, though hopefully few
shall need more than its preventative services.

The Glasgow Humane Society has served the people of Glasgow and the
surrounding areas well for almost 200 years.

Chapter 1

The Clyde in Mourning

Birth – heralded by torrential rain, overflowing burns, filling valleys and swelling the waters of the River Clyde till it surged in one of the worst floods this century.

Death – mourned by the clouds above Glasgow, rainwater over the dark city tenements, submerged roads,and a flooded river.

A lifespan between, a life on and by Glasgow's waterways, fighting against, working with, hating, enjoying, respecting the water and its currents, eddies, flows, hursts (rapids), weirs, locks, learning from, and competing against, the unexpected – a lifespan that was a lifeline to hundreds.

Benjamin Parsonage, BEM, Officer of the Glasgow Humane Society, whose life was synonymous with the river Clyde, died on Monday October 1st 1979, early in the morning, in his house on Glasgow Green near to his beloved Clyde. The suddenness and unexpectedness of his death, coupled with the feeling of total emptiness that we felt in our lives, brought grief we shall never lose. It is hard to remember those days after his death, leading up to the day of his funeral, but they passed and the Thursday arrived.

The garden of the house was covered with wreaths and flowers, many in the colours of the clubs, societies and individuals that they represented. Ben was laid out in the front room with his oars, medals, and the little things he cherished around him. In the rooms of the house, the hall, and even out into the garden, the closest of friends and relatives congregated for the short family service, after which the coffin was carried out by bearers representing every walk of life. Mr. Patrick Barnes-Graham, Chairman of the Glasgow Humane Society, walked in front carrying the family wreath, in the form of a life belt and anchor. The rain was torrential, but did not deter the crowds.

Leading the cortege was a marked operational patrol car from the Eastern Division Police, followed by a plain blue car conveying the Police Chiefs, then two mounted officers, the hearse, the flower cars, and the family cars. As we moved off slowly, other mounted Police Officers saluted in tribute. The cortege passed Nelson's Column, the Doulton Fountain and out of the park through the gate at the foot of Turnbull Street, where the park workmen formed a guard or honour on each side of the pathway.

People crushed into doorways, tried to shelter beneath over-hanging ledges from the downpour, or watched from behind windows, as the funeral director in his black top hat and tails slowly paced St Andrew's Square ahead of the cortege, the only noise the clip-clop of the police horses, the gentle purr of the engines, and the splashing of the rain in the puddles. The cars came to a halt outside the church, and the people who had braved the rain stood silently as the coffin was carried up the steps past, on the left a row of Police Chiefs, some of whom Ben had known as raw recruits to the force, on the right the mounted police and officers from the patrol cars.

Inside the historic St Andrew's church, a packed congregation reflected Ben's friendship with prince and pauper alike, as Knights of the Realm rubbed shoulders with the down-and-outs. The pews were filled, and more were standing in the side aisles and at the back: people from every walk of life. No one will ever know just who was represented in the church.

The service was very moving. It was conducted by a close friend of the family, the Reverend John Logie of Oyne, Aberdeen. A very moving tribute was given by Sir James Robertson, the Chief Constable of the City of Glasgow Police, and Peter Mallan, the tenor, sang, accompanied by Elizabeth, Ben's elder daughter on the organ.

Sir James's speech no doubt echoed the sentiments of most of the mourners:

Relatives, friends and admirers of the Parsonage family, we are assembled, with great sadness in our hearts, each to pay his or her personal tribute to a worthy citizen of Glasgow, whose passing is mourned today in many homes in this country and far beyond. Indeed, in this large congregation there may be some who owe their life to Ben Parsonage. As one who worked closely with him for many years and who therefore had many opportunities of assessing the value of his great work, it is a great privilege to me to be invited to be your mouth piece to pay tribute to a great man – not in stature – but certainly one with a great and kindly heart. He was a pocket Hercules with indomitable courage, mingled liberally with the milk of human kindness, and he had to display, all these qualities frequently in his humanitarian and dangerous work on, and in, the rivers and other waterways, since his first rescue when but a youth of 16 years, 60 years ago.

Throughout these 60 years, in all kinds of weather Ben answered the call of hundreds of human beings in danger, at times displaying almost incredible heroism, and with little thought of his own personal safety. It is the proud and praiseworthy claim of the Parsonage family that the telephone was never allowed to go unanswered.

Many of those rescued were the victims of accident, but others alas, felt they could no longer endure life, and had sought to escape from it in the murky waters of the river. Then it was that Ben and his dear wife showed their Christian charity, their understanding and love for people who had reached that

20

state of mind, by providing to them the comfort, advice and care which were needed. The happy Parsonage home has had to deal with these tragedies of community life. Many were given, in that Christian home, the inspiration and courage to face again the outside world.

Ben often said that he loved boats and that he loved the river, which he so often had to fight. But this modest, unassuming, God-fearing man could also justifiably have added that, above all, he loved his fellowmen and was ready to risk his own life for them. Surely that was Christian behaviour of the highest order.

He suffered his greatest sorrows when he had to recover a child's body, and he was often to be seen in tears, carrying the dripping body of a drowned child. Ben spent his life doing just what he wanted to do, that was, in helping people and saving lives. His bravery on specific occasions was recognised by Her Majesty, with the award of the British Empire Medal, and by the Corporation of Glasgow, in the award of three Corporation Bravery Medals.

Little over a year ago his 50 years of service in the Glasgow Humane Society were publicly recognised by the citizens and organisations in Glasgow, and we little thought then that death was so relatively near. But the existing record of what he has done for mankind in Glasgow, although so impressive, is only a fraction of the whole story of his work on earth. The city's loss is great, but to Mrs Parsonage and her family, who adored him for his many sterling qualities and his great courage, the passing of a beloved husband and Father is shattering.

What lessons can we learn from the life of Ben Parsonage, styled variously throughout his life as 'Guardian of the River', 'King of River Rescues' and many other titles of an affectionate nature?

He has shown to me that, as Christians, we cannot afford to live only for ourselves, and that we should be ready to help others to bear their burdens. His life has also shown to me that we should be prepared to perpetuate what he considered must be treated with wholesome respect, and that, as adults, we should be prepared to warn off young children playing their games unsuspectingly on the banks of the waterways.

Like Tom Bowling in the song of that name:
> 'Faithful below Ben did his duty
> and now he's gone aloft.'

But Ben's living will not have been in vain if we copy his principles to:
> 'Do our best for one another
> Making life a pleasant dream
> Helping some poor weary brother
> Pulling hard against the stream.'

And so, Mrs Parsonage and members of your family, this large congregation of admirers of your dear husband and Father offers to you our deepest sympathy in the grievous loss which you have sustained.

May God be with you in your dark hour.

George, Ben, Elizabeth, Sarah and Anne

As we came from the church, a piper played the 'Flowers of the Forest'. We made our way down Turnbull Street into the Green through the still waiting ranks of park workers. This time the cortege moved along the riverside path, past the rowing clubs, where his Clydesdale Club flag flew at half mast, and members of the club stepped forward to take a last salute at the pavement edge.

We moved slowly along past our boatshed, where Father's best boat, the one with which he saved so many lives, lay: for the first time since he built it, away from its place of readiness, with the oars backwards in its rowlocks, and the ropes on his equipment stark white, in contrast to the colour they were when used for work in the river. The Union Jack flew at half mast from our shed flag pole. As the cortege passed our house, the cars containing the women veered off, leaving the men to make their way to the Rutherglen Cemetery.

The rain was so heavy that the cortege was almost stopped by floodwater as we passed Polmadie Bridge. It was uncanny, as though the elements were sad.

The whole route was lined by police officers, whose white gloves rose in salute as the coffin passed. Mill Street, Rutherglen was blocked by a police car, and officers of many ranks froze to attention as the hearse turned into the graveyard.

After a short service, the pall-bearers lowered the coffin into the grave, but, incredibly, Father did not go down into earth, he went into *water*: the grave was flooded, the coffin floated, and for the first time in those dark days I felt myself smile, for I know that Father would have enjoyed that.

Several wreaths were laid by persons unknown after we had departed, for next day we found them at the foot of the grave.

So Benjamin Parsonage, BEM, was finally laid to rest, on a hillside overlooking the Clyde and Jenny's Burn where, almost 50 years earlier, he had entered a culvert and performed what he himself considered one of his most dangerous deeds.

The next day the sun shone over the city, and witnessed another strange happening. The gates of the Tidal Weir jammed open, and the level of the river Clyde dropped until it was hardly a stream in the middle. I remember someone saying that they could not imagine Bennie without the Clyde, or the Clyde without Bennie, and it certainly seemed that the Clyde did not want to stay, when 'its Guardian Angel' (as the papers had proclaimed him) was no longer there.

My grandmother always wondered about her son's love for the Clyde, for on the day he was born the Clyde flooded – one of the worst floods this century – and now that he had died the river tried to run away.

But the gates went down, and new water entered the river, enough to allow the Saturday regatta to take place. There was talk of postponing it, but Father loved his rowing and would not have wanted that, so the event went ahead, with the programme carrying a small, but touching, obituary.

It was days later before I felt that I could open up our boatshed, and on entering I discovered that the electricity was shut off. I had given the keys of the shed to one of our friends from the rowing club to allow those waiting outside the house before the funeral to shelter from the torrential rain, and when he had locked up at a few minutes to twelve noon he had switched the power off at the mains, causing the electric clock to stop. So for the duration of the funeral and the few days after, time stood still in the boatshed Father had built and worked in.

Ben as a child at Strathclyde Primary School (Front row, second from left)

Chapter 2

Putting Together the Pieces

Father didn't really keep records, but since his death I have had access to his most private belongings. I have looked through old diaries with scribbled notes; addresses, on bits of paper, of children whom he rescued, then sent for the parents to take them home; notes on the hire of lorries to transport his boat to take him to some waterway to recover a body. These – sometimes few – words on the corner of a page have enabled me to work out some astonishing facts: for instance that Father rescued more than 1,000 persons, not the 300 I thought, but no one will ever know the real number.

I am only now beginning to realise the dedication that Father possessed, the total devotion of his life to the Humane Society, the quality and the quantity of his work. One has to realise that in his day there were no special Police Search Units to look for stolen goods, motor cars, or items wanted in connection with some murder hunt. There were no 'walkie-talkies', Land Rovers, trailers, outboard motors, just dedication, courage and hard work. Father will never be replaced; we of my generation have seen the end of an era; a piece of Glasgow history has vanished for ever; it will never be the same again; but as long as water flows down the Clyde and people throng its banks, he will be remembered.

Let me move back in time. A lot of water has passed under the bridge outside our house since the day my maths teacher looked up over his wooden, high desk, and shouted at me as I walked into the classroom leaving the door ajar: 'Parsonage, were you born in a park?' I can remember that day vividly, although, naturally, I cannot remember any of the happenings of the 15th day of October 1943, when I was born in the Glasgow Humane Society House, Glasgow Green, which allowed me to reply 'Yes, sir!'

My mother was Sarah, and my father, Benjamin. I was to be named George. My first involvement with my father's work occurred the very day after my birth. 'Get your evening paper here', the boy shouted, at Glasgow Cross, to the passing public. An old lady bought her paper and took it home to read: 'Born to Sarah Mulholland and Benjamin Parsonage, a son'. Next day, the old lady made her way across the park to the house I was to learn to love and know so well, came to the bedside where Mother cradled her son, and presented a cake that she had baked.

The old lady, whom I have never known, told Mother that Father had given her back the life of her son by rescuing him from the river, and she was delighted to give a small thanks for Bennie's son.

We all learned to row as soon as, or perhaps even before, we could walk. It's one of those things: it's like being able to eat. I can't remember when I couldn't row.

I went to John Street Primary School in Hozier Street, Bridgeton, and was escorted there and back every day by Mother. This wasn't just the usual 'mother-looking-after-the-children' routine, because I soon learned one of the drawbacks of living in the middle of a park was that Father would let none of us cross the often lonely acres of the Green on our own. Even now, if my sister is out, she states a time of return, and I arrange to meet her at the bus stop, or if she is coming by car, I watch for her entering the park to make sure that no one stops her. However, each of us in the family, I think, would rather walk through the Green alone on a dark night than walk up closes or through back-courts. I think we felt safer in our own territory; we believed, and still believe, that very little trouble takes place in the Green, but Father never gave things a chance to go wrong. This meant that, as children, we didn't go across the park to play with other children, or stay behind after school to play games: we hurried straight home.

Still, we had a vast area to play in, and plenty of pals came home with us. We had a large garden in which Father built a sand pit and swings, and, of course we had the boats: what children could want more? It's true we never went out, say, to the pictures, as a family, never went shopping as a family, and on holiday we went with Mother: Father was always on call.

In later years I learned that Father's childhood was very much like mine as far as time spent at the boats was concerned, both spending every minute, when not at school, at the riverside; the only difference was that Father, as a child, had to run further to get home at bedtime than I did.

We had, as children, a great time around the boats, but occasionally, strange things would happen which I was to realise, later on in life, were to do with Father's work. One minute we would be playing happily at the boats, the next we would be ushered without explanation into the house, or Father would lock us up in the boatshed so that we couldn't see what he was doing.

On some of the occasions when we were sent to the house, I would sneak away from Mother to our hall window, which had a perfect view of the road in front of the boats, and tell her when the 'orange box' arrived (the 'orange box' was my childish name for the plain, boxwood coffins used in those times).

Little did I know at that age how serious this business was. As I grew older, Father would give me a telling off for small things, like climbing the fence at the boatshed instead of opening the gate, playing inside the boat compound, or walking along the banks instead of down the road on the outside of the fencing. Gradually, we were all brought up to realise that these things were dangerous, and how could Father tell other people off for doing these things if his own children did them?

Often Father would leave home and his boats day after day, week after week, only returning to the house to sleep. This was when he was away searching for the body of someone who had drowned or was reported missing. When this occurred we learned to play on the road in front of our boatshed and, firstly, to tell Mother if any children, or anyone else, entered our compound or went too near the river elsewhere; then, as I got older, I learned to chase children younger than myself away from the river's edge.

Father was always completely devoted to this prevention of accidents; to an outsider it may at times have seemed fanatical, but his family and those who got to know him closely realised that his actions could often have meant the difference between life and death. Father would row for miles to retrieve a football kicked accidentally into the river, just to make sure no one fell in trying to get it; if he saw an old, burst football in the river he would collect it, cut it up and sink it to make sure that children, not realising that it was burst, wouldn't fall in trying to get to it. It was the same with broken, discarded toys thrown in; oil drums, empty beer kegs, planks of wood: all sorts of flotsam and jetsam were collected and disposed of so that children would not be able to use them to build rafts. All this was slowly and surely drummed into us as children.

There was always plenty to do in those early years: up in the morning; perhaps out for a sail on the river with Father while he was checking things out or picking up a lifebelt, then off to school; home for dinner; back to school; home to the boats. Father never stopped working: building and repairing boats and oars. Going off with the police for hours or days at a time, he kept the garden in far better condition than I have ever been able to, growing vegetables and keeping hens. He did all the the running repairs to our large house (which in itself was no mean feat); he hired boats and laid the buoys and stake boats for regattas: one can now only wonder at the pace and intensity, coupled with incredible skill, that he put into everyday work, from dawn till dusk, and often through the night.

Every year we went down the Clyde coast on holiday. Father saw us off, and that was that. We saw him again when we returned. We had great times as children on holiday, but it is strange to look at family snaps with father in barely any of them.

It was only in the last few years, when I presume that I had matured enough in his eyes to be left 'in charge' at home, that Father ventured away for a few days with Mother and my sisters. It was strange how he enjoyed those days, yet deep down you could tell that he was like a duck out of water when away from his beloved Clyde.

I remember one day he went off in the car with Mother, one of my sisters driving, for a few hours relaxation. The phone rang: 'Is Bennie there?' the policeman asked. 'I'm afraid he is out just now, this is his son George speaking,

can I help?' I was asked to go down to Renfrewshire, where a young girl was missing, and thought to have fallen into the River Cart.

I went there, and had only been searching for a few minutes when Father arrived. His sixth sense had not let him go away settled for his afternoon drive, and he had asked my sister to return home. He had missed my departure for Renfrew by only a few minutes and had followed on down. This was a happy case because Father had only started to search for a few minutes when a policeman further down the river banking found the little girl sound asleep in the long grass.

That little story was only to emphasize the fact that Father didn't like to stray far from his post, but this sixth sense that I mentioned followed him all his life, and there are numerous examples of this, many of which I will tell later in my story. Let me, for the time being, retrace my thoughts to childhood. I mentioned the holiday snaps without Father. This was also the case at weddings and other family or social functions. Those that we did attend we went to on our own for Mother wouldn't leave home if Father was on a case so she would be there to answer the phone and operate the medical room in the event of another emergency. Yes, we soon learned that we only saw our dad when we were at home, and then, mostly at the boats.

Mother did a fantastic job bringing us up. How she managed with the children, the housework of such a large building, the continual secretarial work of answering phone calls, and the nursing work of undressing and looking after persons whom Father had rescued from the river, I'll never know. Father and Mother were really well-matched, not only in their love for each other and in their wish to help others, but also in their capacity for work.

Father tried hard to keep us children as far removed as possible from the sad, and often ugly, side of his work, but the extent of the family involvement was so total that this was more or less impossible. Also, Father had trained me so well that few policemen could row our boat as I could, and it was only a matter of time before I was asked to row his boat on a case. I was 15 years old. There had been a drowning accident at Bothwell Bridge, where boys playing on a raft had fallen in and one had been drowned. It was a lovely summer's day when we hitched our boat to the police van and headed into Lanarkshire.

It all seemed a great excursion at first, far removed from the grim circumstances we were involved in, as we chatted to the policemen about day-to-day happenings; to me it was a new experience, almost a day out. We arrived at the locus and put our boat in the water. Father was told that the police had acquired the services of a sub-aqua club who had carried out a search. The police had also been dragging the river, but the body had not been found, and it was thought that it must have been swept away by the current.

I have heard from Father's friends over the years, how he often did the apparently impossible, of how he succeeded when everyone else had failed, and I have now witnessed this for myself on numerous occasions, but this was the first time I saw it. After a short search in the area around the raft, the area already searched, Father recovered the boy's body. I don't really remember how I felt at that time: grief at the tragedy, seeing my first dead body, proud of my father's prowess. I don't know; one could always sense, even after years of this kind of situation, how sad Father was when he recovered a child's body, but for myself in those early years I cannot honestly state my feelings, my mind is just blank.

We prepared to return home. One of the police chiefs told Father that there had been another drowning tragedy at Motherwell, this time a boy had drowned while swimming. The policeman telephoned Motherwell and asked if they required Father's help while he was in the area, only to be told that sub-aqua units were in attendance, and Father's help would not be needed, but later in the day, the Motherwell Police phoned and asked father out. Next morning, shortly after arriving at the flat sandbanks of the Clyde at the Motherwell park, he recovered the boy's body. So much happened in those two days that I was well and truly initiated into the work of the Humane Society.

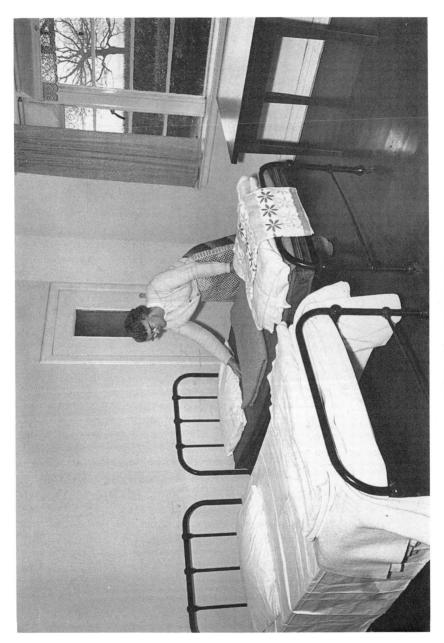

Mother in the recovery room

At the Boats

After that first case in early 1958, whenever I was at home Father took me along to row his boat. I soon learned some of the small but important aspects of his work: that he used a small boat to be as near to the surface of the water as possible; that one had to try to row the boat as smoothly as possible; to row alongside quay walls with three feet of an oar on one side and eight feet on the other side; to row a boat steadily across a river in a heavy current. I was taught to manoeuvre his boat in a manner I never thought possible. One of Father's feats was to move a boat sideways across river in a heavy stream without drifting down river, a skill I have never really mastered; only those who have done a lot of rowing will appreciate what I mean. I learned so much about boat handling that I could fill a book on that subject alone, and even after more than 20 years of helping Father, he was still teaching me about the handling of boats.

Father was probably the fastest oarsman ever to put foot in a boat on the Clyde. I have been Scottish Sculling Champion many times, and won medals outside Britain, yet I could never match the times that Father achieved. One or two friends from his old rowing days kept a note of some of his times, and they are a constant reminder to me that I was never that fast myself, and also show that, although height and weight are of great advantage in rowing, they are not essential for one to row quickly. When he used to hire boats during races he would row his old 21-foot sculling boat, which is still in regular use, with all his clothes and dungarees on, pockets full of hammers and other boat-building tools, whistle in his mouth to blow at any boat that was in the rowing course, down ahead of fours, one race after another – a feat that few could equal.

In the 1920s Father was a member of the Clydesdale Rowing Club and won the 'Fleming Shield', the Sculling Championship.

It was one of the happiest moments of my life when I also won this shield, to follow in his footsteps. The pity was that Father was reckoned a 'professional' when he took the Humane Society job full-time. Some of his friends said that this was the greatest compliment to his rowing ability that they could pay him, but it was sad as some of the old men around the boats in those early years said that they would have backed Father against anyone in the world.

Those of you who know the St Andrew's Suspension Bridge on Glasgow Green will have seen that there are gates at each end of the bridge. I have never seen these gates closed or locked, but Father told me that there were often so many spectators thronging the river banks who wanted to go onto the bridge to watch the racing that the gates were closed to supporters during the races, and only those who genuinely wished to cross were allowed through.

B

Ben with the 'Fleming Shield'

Although in a way I feel that Father always had a 'chip on his shoulder' about not being allowed to compete he always remained completely faithful to his sport, helping clubs whenever possible: sending them new members from the boat hirers; laying their stake boats and buoys for races; looking after their use of the river; helping them when they got into trouble, and taking them from the water when they fell in. (Father would go to great lengths on occasions when oarsmen fell into the Clyde to stop these stories getting into the papers as this could have a detrimental affect on the membership of the club.)

Several stories stick out in my mind regarding this. On November 3rd 1965 an incident occurred involving a rowing club. The following were just some of the headlines: 'Friends see rower swept away by strong current', 'Student saved in Clyde weir drama', 'Student saved in river terror', 'River plunge student saved'. One report read:

'A young Glasgow University student clinging to an upturned skiff was rescued yesterday as he was being swept down a swollen river towards a weir. A 19 year old engineering student was only 200 yards from the raging weir and certain death on the River Clyde at Glasgow Green when he was pulled from the water into a boat by Mr Ben Parsonage of the Glasgow Humane Society. Seconds later his skiff was sucked under the weir gates and smashed to pieces. The student, a member of the Glasgow University Rowing Club, had been practising when his racing skiff overturned. What had been a normal rowing practice day on the river turned into a nightmare. Two other students in another boat tried to go to his aid but their craft also overturned in the powerful current which was running about 9 mph and they just managed to scramble on to the bank themselves. The students' plight was seen by Mr Parsonage's 21 year old son George from their house window beside the river. Together they ran from the house and jumped into the lifeboat and set off. They rowed frantically for 400 yards and just managed to reach him in time, the youth was about 50 yards in front of them. He was clinging to his skiff with one hand and trying to edge towards the bank with the other, seconds later and he would have been washed away. Mr Parsonage who has taken part in more than 200 rescues on the river said later, 'It was the closest thing that I have seen. With the river in its present state after all the heavy rain he would not have stood a chance. He would have been sucked down under the weir gates along with his boat.' His son George added, 'The current was very strong and it took some powerful rowing to catch up with the scull.' Mr Parsonage said that he repeatedly told members of the rowing clubs not to practise on the river when it was in this state. He was only about 200 yards from the weir in which no swimmer would have survived. If he had not been spotted from the window he would not have stood a chance. The student said, 'If I had tried to swim for it I'd have drowned. I just hung on to the boat and hoped that help would reach me before I reached the weir.'

St Andrews Suspension Bridge

Dougie, a sculler from Stirling, was renowned for falling in. Father followed all sculling races just in case, but he kept really close to Dougie. It became a joke among us whether Dougie would complete the course or not. On this day, Dougie and I were racing neck-and-neck down the last straight of the race and, as we passed Nelson's Column, Dougie did his usual trick of falling in and Father did his usual trick of lifting him out. It wasn't till days later that I found out that Dougie had 'blacked out' while racing, and didn't remember anything until Father pulled him into the boat. this shows that you never know when the simplest of recoveries could be a serious affair. Dougie was a very good sculler and, as one of his clubmates said, if he had been able to stay afloat during his races he could have done really well!

There are so many stories about rowing clubs that I could not relate them all. Some funny, like the boat that broke in two, or the oarsman whose oar caught a buoy and who promptly did a beautiful pole vault into the river, some serious, like the four who were caught across the weir gate in a heavy flood, or the sculler who went through the weir, all, fortunately, saved by Father's prompt actions. Our phone was always busy over the years, phoning the police about boys pitching stones at the oarsmen.

Father's love of rowing and regattas was so great that in the family we jokingly say that, because he had to leave a regatta for an hour to visit hospital when my elder sister was born he arranged for Ann and myself to be born in the Green and so not disturb his race day!

Yes, the rowing clubs on the Clyde have a lot to thank Father for.

```
                                   Glasgow University Boat Club,
                                   Men's Union,
                                   University Avenue,
                                   GLASGOW, W.2.

                                   8th November 1965

B. Parsonage, Esq.,
Glasgow Green,
GLASGOW.

Dear Sir,

   On behalf of the Boat Club I would like to thank
you for your very efficient rescue of Jan deVriess
last Tuesday morning.

   There can be no doubt that a very serious
accident was averted by the promptness shown by
yourself and by George. I can only say that all
the members of our Club appreciate your timely
intercession.


           Yours faithfully,

                  J. Michael McMahon.

                  J. Michael McMahon.
                  HON. SEC. G.E.B.C.
```

CHAPTER 3

The Reticent Hero

There were so many aspects of Father's work that he did not want to talk about for one reason or another. The reasons he gave me were: 'Lest I be thought boastful', 'Because of their ugly side', 'Because they may bring hardship to the persons or to their relatives', or 'Because the incidents were treated like something out of National Security, MI5 and all that, and were just not talked about'.

'Lest I be thought boastful' – 'Ben Parsonage', 'Daddy', 'the Gaffer', the character we would all do well to emulate; however I knew him I can only wonder at his feats of endurance and disregard for his own safety: not a foolhardy disregard, but a cold, calculated one. That may seem strange, but if you think of it, many people when faced with possible death can be brave out of sheer fear, but it takes a rare type of courage to calculate, work out your every move, knowing that it may be your last. I am sure that some readers have experienced this, I hope that most haven't, but to do things that, for a 'mere human' (please excuse the cliche), would mean certain death to recover a dead body in order to relieve the minds of the relatives (you would have to have suffered the terrible nightmares and agony of having a close relative missing, dead, but without a body to bury, to understand), or to enter the river, *knowing* the dangers (and that's the important point, people do things on the spur of the moment and without realising the dangers, Father acted knowing full well that he might not come out): this takes a person with a kind of bravery and dedication that I am sure few generations have had the privilege of having among them.

All this was performed in as quiet a manner as possible: not for him a conspicuous uniform; how many reporters can say that they have a photograph of anything but his back or an upturned collar hiding his face?

He shunned publicity for many reasons, but the one that I understand most of all was when he said that if one gets too much publicity for doing things that the public call 'heroic', then people come to expect them of you and, in fact, expect you to be able to do even more: they come to expect the impossible. Often after a heroic rescue he would slink home to get dry clothes and a plate of Mother's soup rather than go to hospital or a police station, or put himself into a position where reporters or others would be able to ask questions or take photos. He hated the limelight. He wished to do his work, do it well, and nothing else.

Because of the ugly side – I really don't know what to say here because we were brought up to say nothing of the horrors that can sometimes occur in drowning because this may bring more sorrow to the relatives of anyone drowned, but I think Father's story would be incomplete without some mention of the gruesome and heartbreaking cases he dealt with.

A dead body goes to the bed of the river and stays there until decomposition sets in. This was one of the reasons why Father spent hour after hour trying to recover a body as soon as possible, for the relatives' sake. If a body is trapped say by silt, or jammed under some sunken object, it does not rise during decomposition as it should but stays under and decomposes further, and finally breaks away from what is holding it down to rise to the surface in a horrific state, often in pieces. Bodies in this state are so bad that they have to be handled very carefully to allow any chance of identification. One I remember was only identified because he had a wooden leg and a wooden arm. Another had sunk to the bottom; along came an iron ore ship, it tied up at the quay wall; at low tide it sat down on the bottom and squashed the body flat. When it came up to the surface it hardly resembled a human being.

Sometimes people committing suicide would slash their wrists or cut their throats to make sure they would die; some tied their hands together, tied their shoe laces together, or tied themselves to large boulders to make them sink immediately. Another man was only identified because a partial dental plate found in the house of a missing person fitted perfectly. Other bodies were hit by passing ships and had their faces split open by propellers; some were murder cases with terrific wounds. There is nothing so terrible as the sight of a bloated, disfigured body, and the smell is indescribable. I have frequently seen policemen who had previously witnessed horrible motor accidents, etc. being sick at such a sight.

The following article written by Detective Chief Superintendent William Muncie QPM, Lanarkshire Constabulary, gives an excellent example of Father's involvement in this type of work.

COMMON SENSE AND DETERMINATION

Always present in the detective officer's mind when called to the scene of a suspicious death is the query – murder, suicide or accident? He is faced with a body and seldom with any facts or information at that time as to the deceased's actions immediately prior to death. The responsibility of reaching a satisfactory conclusion weighs heavily upon him.

The case which I am about to relate occurred some 16 years ago when I was a sub-divisional inspector and was one of the few where some facts were available and a body was expected to be found. I did not, therefore, suffer the same apprehension of some vile deed having been committed as did others when eventually the body was found.

The case concerned a man of about 25 years of age, who was his mother's sole companion and comfort. He had been feeling unwell and depressed for some weeks, and one afternoon he left home telling his mother that he was going for a walk, He did not return.

Late on the day of his disappearance his mother reported to the police the fact that he had not returned. She was very distressed. I caused a search to be made in the locality; the search continued next day and was extended to an area wherein there was a water-filled disused stone quarry with a perpendicular face along one end rising 25 feet above the water. The ground from the ends of this face sloped towards water level and directly opposite the face was a small beach of some 10 feet in length. The water at the wall was estimated as being 20 feet deep and with the wall facing north, it looked a dirty, cold, grim place. A young constable engaged on the search around the quarry reported to me that he had found a medicine bottle on the flat ground a few yards from the edge of the quarry face and at the edge of the quarry face the sparse grass bore signs indicative of some person or animal having lain there. The medicine bottle was very clean and fresh and bore the label of a proprietary make of tonic syrup. It was shown to the mother, who identified it as being similar to one which should have been in the house, but which was now found to be missing. It had contained quite some quantity of the tonic.

I examined the quarry edge and confirmed that the grass did show signs of something heavy having been on it for an area of about 4 square yards right to the edge of that sheer drop. Those facts, together with the thought of the woman's distress being probably due to mother's instinct, had me about convinced that the missing man was in that evil looking water-filled quarry and I was soon to be pleased indeed that I had taken such a close interest and active part in the case, thus getting the proper 'atmosphere' of it. I contacted Mr Benjamin Parsonage of the Glasgow Humane Society and told him of my suspicions that a young man was in the water.

Ben is a great friend of police officers, in and for many miles around Glasgow and is known to them as being extremely devoted to his job in which he has acquired vast knowledge in the locating and removing of bodies from water, and also as a man of infinite patience and determination. He did not hesitate to assist me and I arranged to have a boat brought to the quarry.

No matter how grim or serious a situation faces police officers, flashes of humour always seem to come to the fore and I think this is something we should appreciate and be very happy about. Humour in this case came in the process of off-loading the boat from the vehicle to the water, and it came in the loud Highland accent of a sergeant but let me say it was not in ignorance, but in devilment. Ben was manoeuvring the boat with several policemen, when he said loudly 'Stern first, Sergeant.' came the humour: 'Ben, just cut out the technical terms. Is it the sharp end or the blunt end you want?' With a police officer at the oars, Mr Parsonage began his grim and difficult task of grappling, hampered greatly by the fact that being on the edge of a large, heavily populated area, the quarry, we were soon to find, seemed to have been a favourite place for drowning dogs in a weighted sack. Patiently, all that day, he worked; toward the end of the next day he made a touch with his grappling irons, a touch, which, because of his long experience, he believed was a human body. He returned on the third day and within a short time he brought to the surface a body bound around with a rope and with a hood tied over the head. There were gasps from those present, and then came the talk of murder. I had the body removed exactly as it was to the mortuary at Divisional Headquarters, but, while awaiting transport, I had made careful examination and saw that the rope was in one piece, starting at the ankles and bound around the body. The elbows were embraced by the rope and tucked close to the chest with the hands at the throat and at the sternum was the only full and final knot. The hands were also in a position to have tied the string holding the hood over the head, and the hood, I assumed, was a cushion cover which had been halved diagonally.

I dispatched an officer to the missing man's home to check if a rope was missing and to check the house for the other half of the cushion cover.

Soon the procurator fiscal and the forensic professor of that time, together with the detective superintendent and detective inspector arrived. It was with some devilish delight, in my complete knowledge of this case, together with the fact that I was now out of the CID and looking on, that I carefully watched the expressions on their faces as they viewed the gruesome object. Their examination, however, confirmed my opinion; it was convincingly confirmed when it was found that a rope was missing from the house, and stuffed in a cupboard, was the other half of the cushion cover.

Shortly after this incident, tipping of industrial waste commenced at the quarry. Later came tipping of unsuitable material found while earth-moving in motorway construction. As a result there is now a plateau, of some 400 yards square, of this material and about the centre, under several feet of it, lies the top of the quarry, so that the case illustrates the importance of good briefing, the application of common sense by the searchers, as this young constable so ably demonstrated, and the necessity for patience, devotion and determination by those to whom the final ground task befalls, such as was displayed by Mr Parsonage in this case, in which otherwise our "missing" index file, that entry would still be there uncancelled. In Benjamin Parsonage's experience it is a fallacy to expect every human body to rise to the surface; apart from the possibilities of ledges holding it, the state of the person's health, the depth and the temperature of the water can cause the body to remain submerged indefinitely. Had the body not been found, it would now be over 50 feet below the surface. Who knows, this might also save a piece of head scratching by some future archaeologist!

Dreams and Nightmares

No one will really know how much Father was affected by his often sad and grim tasks, but one evening I was sitting talking to him, making a joke of a daft dream I had one night, when one of the bodies recovered from the river climbed into the boat and said 'Hello', when out of the blue, Father told me of this nightmare he had: 'I dreamed that a body, all dripping and decomposed, was walking towards me, and I ran down the stairs and out of the house, slamming the door behind me. I stood in the garden watching the door, and the body walked right through the closed door and kept coming towards me. I ran and ran, no matter where I ran it followed, kept coming at me! Then I woke up – terrified.' That is the one and only time that Father ever divulged such a story.

There were other tragedies, although the following was more like a macabre joke: on Saturday 14th October 1978, at about 5.40 pm, a police car came to the house and we were told that our help was needed at the canal in Maryhill. We proceeded to the spot and found what could have been a body lying over the top of one of the gates of the locks near the old Maryhill Barracks. We launched the boat and roped up the body. It appeared to be that of a male, but mutilated: no lower legs, no arms, no head. We carefully lifted it out onto the towpath. The CID were sent for and a preliminary examination was held. Father and the CID agreed it was not human. As we discussed the possibilities, Father suddenly realised that what we were looking at was possibly a 'dummy' used for target practice, from the war days at the old Maryhill Barracks! The CID agreed and this was later verified.

Unless the death was suspicious and he was called to a post mortem or a court case Father seldom heard the outcome of the methodical, sometimes months-long process of identifying the bodies taken from the river. Father always said that once his work was done he didn't want to pry into people's affairs, so, often he never even heard if the body was identified. It is unlikely that the following bodies were identified, but we don't know.

Father was called to the Forth and Clyde Canal, at a spot where students trying to raise £200 for charity by cleaning rubbish from the canal had found a body. He had a difficult job removing this body from the long reeds where it lay as it had been in the water for several months and was badly decomposed. It was a male of about 18. I was with Father on this case, and again I was amazed at his ability to remove the body without it breaking up.

Another such case where there was little chance of identification occurred when Father was called to the Clyde at Finnieston Street, where a Ford Anglia car had been winched to the surface by a dredger cleaning the river bed, and a human leg was seen hanging out of one of the doorways. Father, aided by detectives, removed the body of a woman minus her head. The car had no doors and no number plates. The body had been in the water for almost a year. Was it an accident? Was it murder? How did it happen? The river holds that secret along with many others.

I have seen Father recover a body which had floated down a river for miles over rapids, and the continual trailing of the feet on the river bottom had caused the feet and lower legs to wear away. For example, on May 22nd 1932 the body of a boy was recovered near Dalmarnock Bridge with the legs missing from the knee down, and once I rowed the boat in the Upper Harbour while Father recovered the body of a man whose feet were missing. Father reckoned that the man had floated downstream through the shallows of the River Kelvin and out into the Clyde.

One day in 1944 Father found a human skull on the banks of the river above Dalmarnock Bridge. After a short search he located the vertebrae of a body, but nothing else was ever found. The remains were calculated to have been in the river for at lest three years. There was nothing to link the head definitely with the vertebrae, and there was certainly no hope of identification, but they must have belonged to someone. Or had two people died there at some time?

One of the most horrible things that can happen is for a body to rise to the surface but lie in a corner of a river, lake or canal, unseen and open to the hot sun, and to the pecking of birds and ducks. This exposure of a body to the sun causes terrible smell and decomposition and this, coupled with the fact that people will go to terrible lengths to try to see a dead body, was the reason that Father kept a body in the river (in cold storage) until the arrival of the hearse.

He recovered newborn babies thrown into the river, human skulls and parts of bodies in sacks. I remember one case where he went to the Kelvin with the city murder squad. A birdwatcher had seen a skeleton sticking up, legs in the air, out of the ice o the river. When the birdwatcher went to tell folk they didn't believe him, so he went back to the river and pulled the shoe, with the bones of the foot in it, from the skeleton. He took the shoe home and, after his tea, he took it along to the police station. Everyone rushed to the river. Working under fire brigade flood-lights, Father started slowly and carefully digging the body from the ice with a pick-axe and shovel. The amazing thing was that birds, and other wildlife had picked the part of the body above the water to completely clean bleached white bones, but the part of the body below the water and ice was perfectly preserved, as if it had been in a fridge. It was horrible. The police chiefs said they wouldn't have believed that Father could bring the body out whole. There are hundreds more really gruesome stories, but Father did not like to talk of them, and I respect his reasons.

Because they may bring hardship to the persons or to their relatives, I think needs no further explanation, but 'like something out of National Security, MI5 and all that, and were just not talked about' – that is a part of the work that is worth a mention, I am sure.

During the hunt for the guns used by the mass murderer, Peter Manuel, the reporters were sure something was going on and were taking notes and photos of all happenings at our house for days before the search actually started on the

Wrapped in canvas, the body is lifted from the canal to be taken for medical examination river, including who arrived at the house, from the postman to the police chiefs, but never did they receive any information from the Parsonage family.

The previous winter had been a bad one for floods on the river and, as frequently happened, two of the wooden barges to which Father moored his boats were damaged. With a high tide and the use of blocks and tackle these barges were floated, then lifted onto the banking behind the boatsheds. They were rested on blocks two feet high to enable Father to crawl underneath to do his repairs. The day did not have enough hours of daylight for Father to work in, and he could be seen with a small electric lamp on about 80 feet of cable extensions, working away under his barges, replanking and caulking late into the night.

I was too young to be of much help to Father at this time, but I well remember him coming in at supper time, his dungarees covered with oil and the filth with which everything that came out of the river was covered in those years, tired but contented after a good day's work.

As a family we were accustomed to Father having a lot of visits from the police, but during the following days I was aware of more than the usual CID presence in the house when home for lunch or in the evening, although I knew never to enquire too much.

Father went out in his boat during those days, searching for something in the river near to King's Bridge, and in the evening he worked away as fast as he could, finishing the repairs to the flooring of his two barges, then proceeding to take the decking, some of which he had just spent hours renewing, off the barges again. Planks were laid down the banks to form a slipway, and when Father finished his speedy repairs the barges were launched into the river. I later learned that these barges were to be used as platforms, from which Father and the CID officers were to search the riverbed using magnets, up at King's Bridge. Father towed the barges there by rowing boat every morning, and back again at night.

I heard the story unfold during breakfast briefings of the CID by their chiefs, held in our dining room. The story of Peter Manuel is common knowledge now, but at that time the name of the murderer and the massive amount of ground work that would have to be carried out before any conviction would be made were known only to a handful of police chiefs. It seemed that Manuel had told the police that he had thrown his gun into the river at a spot about 100 yards downstream of King's Bridge. This was what Father had been searching for. Now, as those who came into contact with him know, Father's knowledge of the river was fantastic, and he had formed the opinion that the gun must be in one of the small holes he knew were on the river bed. They discussed what their next move would be, the police said they could supply magnets, and this led to the work on the barges mentioned earlier. Electricity cables were even laid down to the water's edge to enable the use of an electro-magnet. Father and the CID officers searched as thoroughly as they could. It was amusing, in the morning before I left for school, to see the amount of heavy protective clothing these officers put on in comparison

44

to Father, and how he laughed at them for putting on gloves: 'Gloves just get in the way when you are working with ropes.'

The flasks of hot soup and special tea loaded into the haversacks to sustain the policemen during their work were unfamiliar things to Father, who seemed able to face the elements without such luxuries quite happily. In the evening when I came home from school in time to see the search finishing for the day, they would be trying to get some heat back into their bodies, talking about the freezing water turning to ice on the ropes and even cutting their gloves, and marvelling how Father took all this in his stride, not just for the few days working with them, but week after week, year after year, winter after winter on the river.

There were moments of drama when two guns were brought to the surface, but curiously they were not the ones being sought. One was a small automatic, and the other a tiny lady's pocket, or handbag, gun. It just shows the secrets the bed of the river must still hold!

Verification of how well Father knew his work and the contours of the riverbed came again, only a few years ago, when one of the CID men who had been involved in the Manuel case said: 'They could have found the gun a lot quicker if they had listened to Ben at the beginning and brought in the diver.' At last the arrangements were finalised for a Clyde Trust diver to be brought in, and his boat moved slowly upriver through the winter snows, negotiated the weir, and berthed at Father's wharf. Next day the diving boat moved to King's Bridge where Father told the diver what the bed of the river was like and where he thought the gun lay. The outcome of the search is now history: the gun was found and Peter Manuel convicted. The barges were brought back to the wharf where new decking was laid, and things again returned to 'normal'.

Then there was the day that Father recovered an article wanted in connection with a murder hunt. The newspaper men were listening in to the police radios on the quay wall but Father didn't want them to know anything, so he said to the policeman rowing the boat: 'Do you have the Gaelic?' He did. 'Do any of the police on the quay wall have the Gaelic?' They did, so Father's information was passed to the quayside police, and over the radio to the control room, all in the language of the Highlands. This really baffled the reporters. By the time they found a native Gaelic speaker it was too late, all the action was over. Marvellous, even James Bond hasn't thought of this yet!

There are many cases that I cannot and would not put in print to this day. What amazing control Father had, to be able to keep totally silent about so many experiences, and instill into his family his wish for some of these incidents never to be made public knowledge. My apologies if I make you wish to hear more, I don't mean to tease, but I have to emphasise how strict Father was, once he had given his word that certain occurrences would never be made public from his lips. Some tell their secrets in their memoirs, but many stories remained forever in his memory and were never told.

The dramatic scene aboard the diver's barge in the Clyde today as the gun is found. Diver David Bell has just surfaced and handed the gun to Superintendent Henry Crawford, who is seen inspecting it. On his right is Ben Parsonage, of the Glasgow Humane Society, who has been helping the police. Others on the barge are ready to assist the diver out of his gear.

CHAPTER 4

The Making of a Legend

Father was brought up knowing what hard work was. While he was still at school, he worked from 6 am to 8 am in the cotton mills in Poplin Street, Bridgeton and again from 4 pm to 6 pm. Then, as soon after 6 pm as he could manage to finish his tea, it was down to the boats in the Green.

Bob Davidson, a retired Glasgow policeman and a past member of the Clydesdale Rowing Club, remembers that during the first World War he and his fellow club members greatly admired the ability of the wee boy in short trousers who helped at the boats when he wasn't at school, who was able to jump around the boats, row them, and handle them with an ability far in advance of his years.

One of Father's earliest memories of being at the boats was an incident that occurred around the end of the First World War. Two or three pals were out in different hired boats. One of the lads had a revolver with him, a souvenir brought back from the war by an older friend. He pointed it for fun at the boys in the other boat and, thinking it empty, pulled the trigger. Bang, the gun fired, and one of the boys dropped dead, blood everywhere, because no one had known that there had been a bullet in the gun. Father remembered this vividly, as he was given the job of washing the blood from the boat, called the *Mary*, with a brush and pail.

In 1919 he saw a woman throw herself into the water from the banking near the suspension bridge. He ran along the bank, and plunged into the water to bring the woman to safety. For weeks after this incident, Father noticed that a priest came down and hired a boat regularly. It turned out that the woman rescued was one of his parishioners, and this was his way of showing his gratitude.

On October 4th 1922 Father was involved in a case where two men were drowned when a sling broke as it was being used with a crane to lower their boat into the water, and they were thrown into the river. I have so often seen Father use slings and a crane to lower him and his boat into the water and already I was frightened of this, but when I heard this case and read what could happen, it really drove home the dangers.

During these early years, prior to full-time involvement with the Humane Society, Father took part in many rescues. I am mentioning a few of these to show how, from childhood, he was reared in these affairs.

Boat being lowered into water

On Sunday June 10th 1923 a little boy of 10 fell into the Clyde while running along the sloping bank opposite the Humane Society House. The alarm was raised, and Father and a friend promptly put off in a boat from the barges opposite and picked him out of the water. They took him to the Humane Society House where he was tended to and put to bed until his mother arrived to take him home. The mother presented Father and his friend with a tie each as a token of her gratitude.

In 1923, at 4.45 pm on July 17th, during the Glasgow Fair holidays, a sad boating fatality occurred of the sort which Father, on taking up his post, went to extremes to prevent: a man and his 9-year-old son were drowned near Rutherglen Bridge when their boat capsized and his wife narrowly missed the same fate by clinging to the keel of the boat when it had turned over. It appears that the boy wanted a spell at the oars and stood up in the boat, which lurched, causing him to fall overboard. The father went to grasp the boy and the boat keeled over. The father and son sank almost immediately in each others arms. The mother held on and cried for help. Two men on the south side of the river took off their boots, jackets and vests and swam to the rescue. They were quickly followed by two boats which had been some distance off. The boat and the woman were towed to the north bank in safety, and she was rushed to the Royal Infirmary. Word reached the Glasgow Humane Society House, and Father and a friend rowed to the spot and recovered both bodies in about one and a half hours. This should serve as a constant reminder to all boat users not to change seats while out on the water.

As has happened so often over the years, on Saturday December 15th 1923, at 9.20 pm, a man threw himself into the Clyde from the St Andrew's Suspension Bridge near the Humane Society House. The alarm was raised when a woman witness screamed, a boat shot out from the Humane Society Wharf, and Father rescued the man in the nick of time. With police help he carried the man into the house, where artificial respiration was applied. The man was soon out of danger.

It was about this time that, whilst Father was working in the cellar of the old house, a big, heavy man came along the towpath shouting at the top of his voice, turned right through the sliding gate of the boat yard, and went down the steps tearing his jacket off and telling the world how he was going to swim the river. Father, with no time to lose, sprinted across the road and leapt from the top step of the stairway onto the man's back causing him to fall to the ground, where he managed to pin him until help arrived. The police were called and took the man away.

Shortly after 2 pm on Monday November 12th 1924 another man threw himself from the suspension bridge at Glasgow Green, near the south side, into the Clyde. The river, owing to the prevailing rain, was in strong spate. He was being swirled around by the eddying current when Father sped in a boat from the Humane Society wharf. The would-be suicide was seized, and hauled into the frail boat. The exhausted man was taken to the house, and later sentenced to 14 days' imprisonment for being drunk and causing a breach of the peace. This eddy is one of the most dangerous in the river, and has claimed several lives, including those of would-be rescuers. It is a most dangerous spot to enter the river, though Father had done it many times.

When he left school he worked in a chair factory, then a laundry, before going to serve his time as a boilermaker in the yards. He worked on submarines, torpedo boats, cruisers and destroyers, in the old Blythswood shipyard, and in Beardmore's. There were many idle months during those depression years and Father spent many hours tramping the Bonington Moors and up past the Stoneybyres Falls looking for work. All his spare time was spent at Glasgow Green. For a time Father worked in the old Chalmers Shipyard in Rutherglen, as a heater of rivets. After another short spell of work, this time in the steelworks, he returned to Beardmore's and took up his tools again.

Among his keepsakes I found this payslip:

For those who don't know, a riveter (in this case, Father) employed two other persons, one to heat his rivets, and one to 'haud on' (hold the heavy hammer on the head of the rivets while Father hammered on the other end). That is why the sheet says 'Parsonage & Co'. How wages have changed – £5.8.8 for 3 people's weekly pay, piece work!

On November 11th 1928, a week after finishing his time at Beardmore's, Father moved his belongings, and took residence in the old Humane Society House at Glasgow Green.

On December 23rd 1928 he had the very sad job of recovering the bodies of two wee boys, one 4 and one 6 years old from the canal at Castle Street and at the beginning of January 1929 he recovered the body of a boy who had fallen through the ice on the canal at the White Bridge on Alexandra Parade.

On January 15th 1929 a woman jumped from the St Andrew's Suspension Bridge at the south end, and entered about 18 inches of water head-first, smashing her head on the rocks below the surface. Father rowed quickly across the river and lifted her into his boat. An ambulance was on the scene immediately to take the woman to hospital, but she was found to be dead. Later that year, a woman jumped from the same bridge, but this time into deep water. Father again raced to the scene in his boat. Two boys who were out in a rowing boat rowed over to the woman to attempt to help her, and somehow she managed to cling to their boat. Father came alongside and caught hold of her, but she was so hysterical he could hardly break her grip. Once he had managed to do so, he lifted her into his boat and brought her to the house, where he tended her until the ambulance came to take her to the hospital.

On Monday July 15th 1929 the cry was raised from the boating station on the south bank: 'There's a man in the river at the King's Bridge.' This is the bridge where Govan Street (now Ballater Street) crosses the river about 400 yards

BLYTHSWOOD SHIPBUILDING CO., Ltd.,   **A. R. Dept.**
SCOTSTOUN.

RIVETTERS.

No.

Pay ending

Parsonage & Co

DESCRIPTION OF WORK	No. of Ship	Size of Rivet	Quantity or Number	Rate	Amount		
Web Frames Done in Position	18	⅞	535		4	10	4
Frame Conn Angles to Shlls	"	"	66			11	·
					5	1	11
Plus 25%					1	5	6
					6	7	5
Less 15%					·	19	1
					5	8	4
" 25%					1	7	1
					4	1	3
Plus days allowance					1	4	
" Bonus					6	1	
					4	8	8
					1	-	-
					5	8	8

upstream of the wharf. Father and a friend raced to the scene, but the man had sunk. He dropped his grapnel, and after about 10 minutes picked the man up. He applied artificial respiration in the boat and also at the Humane Society wharf, and kept trying to bring the man to life, but when a doctor arrived he found the man to be dead.

Yes, in 1928 Father had taken on a job which entailed being permanently on call. He carried out his duties faithfully and was very contented to do so. In over 50 years a call for help never went unanswered. I have yet to meet anyone who has given a lifetime of such selfless devotion.

Many a time my mother felt a little sad that he had no social life, but doing his job and doing it well was all he worried about. Mother could not go out and leave the children with Father as he could be called away at any minute. Even she herself hurried over the Green, bought her messages and rushed back, wasting no time, so that if Father had been called out she would be there to keep the treatment room open for any accident and to answer the telephone to keep police or anyone else informed of where to contact Father if he was needed.

On the other hand, there was a lot of happiness. Birthday parties, anniversaries, etc. were all held at home. Even my grandparents' Golden Wedding was celebrated in Glasgow Green. Let me continue the story of Father's work with one of the incidents when he must have felt real satisfaction: an accident prevented.

One autumn evening, just after 10 pm, Father noticed a woman with a baby in her arms, crying her heart out, making her way down the banking of the river. Her intentions were obvious, and Father had to move fast to stop her going into the water. He sat her down in the boatshed and let her pour out her troubles. This brought her to her senses. Father had by this time enlisted the help of two young women; the three of them walked the woman and her baby home, where she promised to make a fresh start. As far as we know, all ended happily.

Jenny's Burn

On December 27th 1929 an incident occurred that was to bring out the factors in Father's character that were to mark him for the rest of his life as a man of intense bravery.

On that fateful Friday, just after dinner time, the water of Jenny's Burn, swollen to a raging torrent by the winter's rainfall, claimed the life of a 10-year-old boy who had, while playing on the banks, lost his footing and fallen into the burn. When his chums raised the alarm, the rescue services swung into action, and raced to the scene, but the boy had disappeared and there no hope of him being brought from the water alive. In fact it was calculated that the boy's body would have been swept into an underground culvert just down river of where he had fallen in. Among those who had raced to the scene, and who now stood on the banking surveying the seemingly hopeless situation, was young Bennie Parsonage. Along with others, he joined in the various attempts that were made to cut a trench and divert the course of the burn, and the attempts to dam the burn.

Notable rivermen tried various methods to recover the boy's body without success. All through the next 9 days, work continued from dawn till well after dusk, with Father always to the fore. The New Year came and went with no one really noticing it, so intense were the efforts to recover the body. During the damming efforts, two helpers were almost drowned when planks gave way, hurling them into the water. One later said 'There being so little room in the burn to swim, I had the greatest difficulty in keeping afloat, and to make matters worse, there was a terrible undercurrent. It was a desperate plight for me, and I could not have escaped from the burn without aid'.

On the tenth day, Bennie Parsonage arrived, as usual, in the early hours of the morning, to discover that some men had managed to hold the water back with a rough dam, and that the five Rutherglen fire engines which were on the scene were managing to lower the water in the culvert and, in fact, there was now a gap between the water level and the top of the culvert. By 9.20 am there were several hundred people watching proceedings.

The search of the culvert was a task fraught with considerable danger, due to the water still flowing through, but Father volunteered to go into the narrow passage. He had offered to make the attempt two days earlier, but, before he was quite ready to enter, the dam burst and within a few minutes the culvert was flooded once more. Had the dam burst a few minutes later, he would have been in the tunnel, caught like a rat in a trap. The father of the victim was standing by, as he had done practically day and night since the accident, having vowed that he would not rest until his son's body had been recovered. At last it was considered time for Bennie to go into the dark culvert. He recounts in his diary:

'I had only gone a few feet in when I hard a shout, and coming out to see what was the matter, was told that I could not be allowed to go without having a rope tied round my waist, in case I should have to be pulled out again. Two ropes were tied around me, but as I found that one hampered my movements, I went into the tunnel with only one rope, which was attached to my waist. Once inside, I could see light from the other end of the culvert, and decided to remove the second rope, so that if anything happened I could try to get out at the bottom end. The dam was built upstream of the culvert, and if it had burst I would have been carried downstream and, hopefully, out at the other end. The rope would only have trapped me more as I entered from the upstream side of the culvert (entry could not be made from the downside due to a bend in the culvert.)'

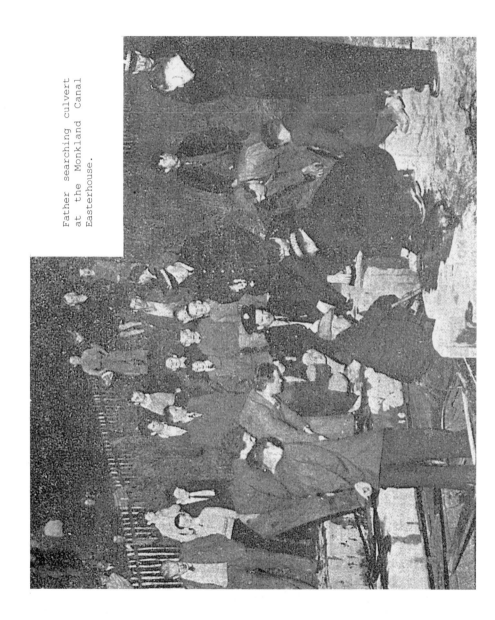

Father searching culvert at the Monkland Canal Easterhouse.

Forty minutes passed after Ben entered the tunnel, every minute seeming like an hour to the waiting crowds. When the dam partly gave way and the bags of clay were washed aside, debris and a torrent of water rushed down into the culvert. The men thought they would not see Ben again, but they repaired the dam immediately. Ben later said:

'I never gave a thought to the danger I was running, as my thoughts concentrated on the work of recovering the body, and I knew that if I did not succeed, the child's body would probably never be seen again. I braced myself against the currents of debris and just kept going. I had walked into the culvert, which was about 60 feet long and 9 feet in diameter, with water up to my chest, for about 40 feet, when I touched something with my pole. I had to work practically in darkness, and it was a case of feeling about until I discovered the body of the little boy. I lost no time in getting out of the culvert. I would not like to think of what might have happened if the second dam had burst while I was inside the tunnel.'

The crowds gasped when Ben appeared at the culvert entrance carrying the body of the little boy in his arms. He then crept away through the crowd, and ran back to his home in the Green for a change of clothes and a cup of tea.

Then there was the day that Father was rowing upriver to search for a parcel that had been dropped off Polmadie Bridge the previous night. The boat was making its way through the south arch of the King's Bridge, Govan Street, when he happened to look around, and saw a man struggling in the water near the north bank. He birled the boat around and raced to the spot, but the man passed just out of reach as he didn't want to be saved. Father dived in and got hold of him, and brought him back to the boat, where both were helped on board. He was brought to the house and thence to Millbrae Mission Home, Langside. This man had embezzled the Anchor Line of £29,000, and wished to do away with himself. He was jailed for four years. Later it was rumoured that this man was living in luxury in South Africa. Four years in jail, followed by such a life, must surely be better than death at the bottom of the Clyde!

On November 20th 1930, Father recovered the body of an engineer from the fishing skiff *St Clair* from Girvan. I wonder if we shall ever again have fishing boats come into the heart of our city?

Just as we shall see few fishing boats from Girvan in our Upper Harbour again, so we shall not see the mills in Poplin Street again, where Father recovered the body of an 8-year-old boy who drowned in the pond in Anderson's Mill. Another feature that has disappeared is the Old Sand Jetty near the Tidal Weir, where a 7-year-old boy was drowned in August 1931.

One Sunday in 1931 Father was asked to go to Dalmarnock Bridge where

Scene of the drowning tragedy at Jenny's Burn Rutherglen, where James
A. Campbell (8) lost his life. Inset is picture of Benjamin Parsonage,
a Bridgeton young man, who yesterday recovered the body of Campbell at
great personal risk.

AFTER TEN DAYS.

BODY TAKEN FROM JENNY'S BURN.

BOY'S FATE.

The body of James Anderson Campbell (10), of 37 Acorn Street, Bridgeton, Glasgow, who fell into Jenny's Burn ten days ago, was recovered yesterday.

A thorough search was made at the time without recovering the body, and it was thought that the boy might have been carried under a culvert at the bridge which passes over the burn at Blackfaulds Road.

The burn was dammed, and several fire engines from Rutherglen pumped water from the culvert.

Yesterday Benjamin Parsonage, of Bridgeton, who has been acting as assistant to Mr. George Geddes, of the Royal Humane Society at Glasgow Green, volunteered to make a search of the culvert, and with ropes attached to one leg and arm he entered the dark tunnel, through which water was still flowing.

His efforts proved successful, for after proceeding about 40 feet he discovered the body of the child.

there was a body in the river. He rowed to the spot, and found the body of a man lying face down in shallow water, about two feet from the bank. Father said that the man could only have been in the water for a few hours, and he thought that he must have stumbled on the towpath and fallen down the banking, stunned himself by hitting his head on the rock, and lay there, to be drowned by the rising tide.

On Wednesday August 5th 1931 the old Glasgow paper *The Bulletin* carried the story of Benjamin Parsonage diving into the river near St Andrew's Suspension Bridge to save a woman who had fallen in. He brought her to the bank and gave her artificial respiration until the arrival of an ambulance to take her to hospital. The paper also recalls that several hundred people watched from the suspension bridge.

Father Confessor

A few days later, Father walked from the house, down the brae towards the river and was amazed to see a girl struggling in the water. He rushed to a boat, and rescued her just in time. She was taken to hospital. I heard Mother and Father talking about this rescue to a friend one evening: 'I rescued a girl who went off that bridge once, she went to the same church as my sister, and she told my sister I gave her the best advice that anybody ever gave her.'

He was a great 'Father Confessor': 'Father Benjamin' Mother used to call him, because in his young days, when he made a lot of rescues – by boat or otherwise – he'd bring the person in and would talk to them. Well, this girl was down in the dumps. She had been coming from her work, her boyfriend had broken off their engagement, and when she got to the suspension bridge at just about tea-time, something came over her and she went into the water. Father got her out and gave her a good talking to. He told her that there wasn't a man alive worth doing that for, that you never know what's in front of you and she would be better off without him. The girl said it was the best advice she was ever given. As far as we know she lived a happy life after that.

On Saturday October 31st 1931 the Humane Society was asked to send someone down to Bridge of Weir to search for a man who had gone missing while fishing in the River Gryffe. Father and a helper, one of his good oarsmen, took the bus there. A local minister on the bus told him roughly where the locus was, and the driver stopped as close to the spot as he could.

The two made their way across open fields on foot to the river. The police were standing on the bank watching the Port Glasgow boatmen searching; there was only one boat, and the Port Glasgow men were in it. The police said 'Oh, they'll manage.' – Father's reply: 'Thanks, I'm away home.' 'Hang on' said the police, 'since you're here, you may as well try.' (the searchers were at this point halting for a break). Father insisted that his own man rowed the boat; after ten minutes' search, they recovered the body.

Saturday January 30th 1932 was such a foggy night that there was visibility of only 2 or 3 yards, yet Father managed to find his way upstream to the 'Bogie Bridge' (so called because there were coal pits, like the Old Farme pit at Rutherglen on the south side of the river, and this bridge was used to take the pit bogies across – all that remains now are four wooden posts) and bring the body back to the wharf. I joke that Father knew the river so well that he could find his way around blindfolded.

Later in the month, Father recovered the body of one of Sir William Arroll's workers, who was drowned at the building of the new quay wall. It is interesting to note that father recovered the body right at the spot where the accident occurred, although Arroll's diver had already been searching at that locus.

Then came a tragedy involving a baby!

BABY'S BODY IN PARCEL
Glasgow Canal Mystery
Ben Parsonage was successful in locating the body of a nine weeks' old infant. The body was in 12 feet of water, it was wrapped in a brown parcel and white shawl – the child had been dead for some time.

During the three days' search of the canal huge crowds have congregated on the canal banks to watch. The mother had drowned the baby in a bath and took it to the canal and wrapped it up with a weight and threw it in.

On April 30th 1933 there was an accident at the tidal weir. A group of young boys were having a picnic on the grassy slopes at the back of the weir – a very dangerous place to have a picnic, although to this day, it remains a popular spot in the summer for adults and children alike, who climb the fence and lie in the grass watching the river. I can't really blame them. It's a lovely spot, and we've said for years that they should move the fence to the top of the sloping bank, and let the public use this stretch of grass safely. People want to sit and watch the river flowing by, so why put the fence 75 to 100 yards away?

The oldest boy fell into the swirling water. Two men waded in up to their necks, but couldn't find the boy, who had by this time sunk. People attempted to launch a boat, but in their hurry, and with the swirling water, it sank. Father had been alerted to the accident, and was racing downstream as only he could. With helpers, his boat was carried speedily around the weir and re-launched. Within a few minutes he recovered the boy's body, but too late to save him.

As Templeton Street was Father's temporary home, there was no telephone, but the Eastern Police Office was almost next door. Anyone requiring Ben's services would phone there, and a policeman would come to the door with a telegram-like message, telling him where he was required. In those days, Father's boat was lifted onto the back of a Bryson's lorry, which transported him to wherever he was needed.

One day in November Father received this message:

TELEPHONE MESSAGE.

From *Supt McLaren, C.I.D.* .... Telephone No. ....

Date *2 : 11 : 33.* ....Hour........ ....Recd. by........

Please tell B Parsonage Humane Society to communicate with Clydebank Police immediately

EASTERN POLICE OFFICE
NOV 1933
GLASGOW

Message attended to by.......... Date.......... Hour..........

Remarks..........

When he did so, he was asked to go to Clydebank to search for a docker who had drowned when the vessel on which he was working with two other men lurched, and threw them all into the water: One drowned and two were rescued. He took a boat down to Rothesay Dock on one of Bryson's motors. After 5 days of constant searching, Father recovered the body on November 7th.

Another unusual event occurred when Father, with Uncle George rowing his boat, was searching for a man who had been seen to fall into the River Clyde at the entrance to Kingston Dock. They searched on into darkness, until, around 1 am on a Saturday morning, they heard shouts for help coming from somewhere above.

They made for the quay wall and climbed up the ladder to find that a constable, who was standing by in case they found the body, had fallen across one of the holes for the bridge runners, and had dislocated his shoulder blade. Father treated the injured man, and made him as comfortable as possible. They shouted across the dock to another constable to phone for an ambulance. He was removed to the infirmary. At 10 am the following morning Father recovered the docker's body.

CHAPTER 5

Templeton Street

Life wasn't always all work and no play, it naturally had its happier moments, as you will see. Mother takes up the story:

Early in 1933 I came down with a girlfriend and my young brother to the boats, and my brother introduced me to Ben. He was at that time a small, dark, slim-built, shy and very serious young man.

I went out with my girlfriend and brother in a rowing boat for a wee while, and when we came back we sat talking, and Ben asked me back down again. After that, any spare time I had was spent at the Green. Ben would take me out in a boat, and we would row between the weir and the King's Bridge. This was so he could listen for the phone and be on hand if he was needed. I couldn't row, but Ben soon taught me. I don't know why, but I just took it for granted that he couldn't come for me, and that I had to come over the Green, as he always needed to be on call. Fortunately, I didn't stay far away. It took me five minutes to get home and, as Ben's brother was around a lot at that point, he was able to stand by for the short time until Ben took me home at night. We had

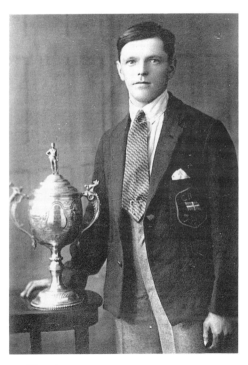

Bennie as a young man

61

'The Winchin!'

lots of fun in those days. Two or three young men who were idle were often around the boats,and told everyone that 'the winchin' was done under the arches of the King's Bridge, and if they cared to look, they would find a big nail that Bennie had put there for hanging up his 'jaicket and bunnet'! At this time, he was living in temporary accommodation at 11 Templeton Street. The Humane Society was having a new house built, as the old one had been condemned. As the winter nights advanced about half a dozen of us went back to Templeton Street. What happy times these were. Ben would send for fish suppers at 3d each! As he lived by himself, the loaf went on the table, the margarine, the bag of sugar, and the milk bottle, and we all thoroughly enjoyed our fish suppers out of the paper.

Of course Ben and I were engaged by this time. We had become engaged on Fair Saturday, and were planning our wedding for Christmas. Guess what? Ben's first thought was to hold the wedding as near his boatshed as he could. The wedding was to take place in the Green, as he never even thought then of leaving the place. It was to take place at the Glasgow Rowing Club on 22nd December 1933, adjacent to his own boatshed. In those days, Bennie shied clear of all reporters, but a young reporter was always around, looking for news, and told Ben he had come up with a great heading: 'Ben takes the plunge', for his article, and he would get a photographer down. Ben told him if he did this he would land in the Clyde himself – camera and all. I think he terrorised the young reporter, who didn't come near, and I now feel it would have been a nice record for the family to look back on.

What a night that was! Glasgow Green rejoiced into the early hours of the morning, and a great time was had by all. The young men at the boats managed to get their bit in by hanging a notice on the bridge which read: 'All intending suicides please leave off till tomorrow.'

You might like to hear a bit more about the wedding: I was all ready and waiting, and wondering what had happened, as the best man and bridesmaid hadn't turned up and the usual teasing was going on that I'd been deserted. Knowing Bennie, I might have been. If a case had come in, I'm sure he would have gone on it. As it was, his brother, who was best man, said they had a job getting him away from the river so he would be dressed in time for his wedding. However, back to the best man and bridesmaid: the taxi driver couldn't find the bridesmaid's address, and this was the reason for the delay. When I arrived at the clubhouse, however, all was well. The minister and all the guests were waiting – and Ben!

Left to right: George Parsonage (Ben's brother), Ruby Hart, Ben, Sarah, Bessie McQeen

After the reception we walked across the Green, home to 11 Templeton Street. What a laugh next morning, when Ben first opened the glass door, and then the storm door, to find sitting on the steps, his brother and a friend with milk and rolls.

But Father didn't even get his breakfast in peace that morning, and there was no time for a honeymoon, for on that Saturday morning, after the wedding, he received a message from the Rutherglen police, telling him that they had found a coat, pipe and spectacles on the bank of the River Clyde, about 50 yards east of Dalmarnock Bridge on the south side; they had been identified as belonging to a Rutherglen man who was missing from home.

Father searched all day Saturday and Sunday without success. While he was

63

c

searching at Rutherglen on the Sunday, the police sent a message to him that a man had disappeared from the docks area around Shieldhall, and it was feared he had fallen in.

On Monday, Christmas Day, while Father was searching at Shieldhall, the police advised him to call off the search as they had no one reported missing. Tuesday came, and Father returned to Dalmarnock Bridge and searched till dark for the missing man from Rutherglen. (This man, sadly, was recovered from the river several weeks later, 5 miles downstream from Dalmarnock).

He returned for his tea, but at 8 pm he was taken in a police car to Cloberhill Bridge, Knightswood to investigate the disappearance of a man in the Forth and Clyde Canal; the police and the bridgeman had searched that afternoon without success.

After surveying the locus, Father made arrangements for a boat to be taken to the canal by one of Brown's motor lorries the following morning. On Wednesday December 27th, at 12 noon, Father recovered the body from the canal and, at last, was able to return home to his first Christmas dinner cooked by his wife. Thankfully, they were allowed to bring in the New Year in peace and quiet.

Early January 1934 brought freezing weather. Work was going on at Adelphi Street, building up the river bank with slag where it had caved in when the weir gave way and the water level fell. A steam wagon loaded with slag was reversing down McNeill Street and backed over the banking into the River Clyde.

It stuck at the edge with its boiler just clear of the river. The fire on the engine was put out by the water, the cabin with the driver in it was almost 10 feet above the surface. If the wagon slipped, the boiler would blow up, and little would be left. Father raced by boat across the river, and drew alongside the precariously balanced vehicle, hoping it wouldn't move. The lorry driver scrambled from his seat, and was helped by Father into the boat. He was none the worse for his experience, but very, very lucky.

During the early months of the year Father's work continued as usual, with accidents occurring in such varied places as the Clyde at Old Kilpatrick, the Hairlaw Dam, Neilston, and the canal at Garngad.

In July 1934 he received a message from the police that a boy of 4 was missing from his home in Castle Street, and it was feared he may have drowned in the Forth and Clyde Canal, near to Kennedy Street. Father took his boat to the canal and, with hundreds of people watching, began his search.

After about an hour, something nagged at Father's brain: something was wrong about the area he was searching. The police sergeant on the bank was chasing away children who wanted to get as close as they could to watch. Father called over one of the boys, and asked: 'Hey son, where would you go to fish?' – 'Roon the back of the Carlton, Mister.' was the reply. The police sergeant said that too many adults frequented that area, which was on another canal – the Monkland.

Now, one has to understand the arrangement of the canals: you could row from one canal to another easily but by land you had to go back out onto the main road, across it, and up the next street to get onto the Monkland Canal bank. Father, being unhappy searching in the Forth and Clyde Canal, lifted his grappling irons and rowed around to the Monkland. The crowd rushed around by the route I have just mentioned, but by the time they arrived on the Monkland Canal bank, the boy's body was recovered. A remarkable incident, but only one of the many occasions when Father's unique sixth sense prevailed.

On August 16th 1934, Father was involved in another strange case. I shall let the newspapers take up the story:

TRAGEDY OF SIXFOLD ESCAPE FROM SCOTS PRISON
Youth drowned in vain swim for liberty
Barlinnie Break thrills large crowds
Five captured after prompt pursuit
A prisoner attempting, with five others, to escape yesterday from Barlinnie Prison, Glasgow, was drowned after plunging into Monkland Canal near-by in a desperate effort to elude pursuing warders. It was thought that he had escaped, but three hours later, learning from the other men who had been captured that he had not reappeared above the water, the prison officials had the canal dragged and found his body.

The dead youth had been in prison since August the previous year.
The other youths who took part in the tragic escapade were recaptured within half an hour and returned to the borstal section of the prison unaware of the fate that had overtaken their companion. Until it was definitely ascertained that the youth had been drowned, police officers furnished with descriptions, searched tirelessly for him throughout the city.

Mr. Benjamin Parsonage recovered the youth's body about 6 pm. The body was conveyed to the mortuary at the Eastern Police Station.

Later that year, in October to be exact, Father was involved in another risky recovery of a body. He was searching at Jamaica Bridge, when he received word that there was a body in the River Kelvin. He telephoned Brown's garage in Templeton Street and asked them to send a lorry to convey him and his boat to Kelvingrove Park. On arrival at the scene, it was discovered that the river was in terrible flood, and Father decided that he could not launch his boat. The body was jammed tight by the flood water against the boulders that form a dam in the river at this point.

He produced a ladder, and layed it from the bank to the top of the dam, over the torrent of water and, taking a rope with him, crawled along rung by rung, until he could lie down, stretch out and tie the body. At any moment the ladder could have broken, but, fortunately, it held him and, body roped up, Father crawled

Sarah with baby Elizabeth

backwards to the banking and, together with the waiting police, he pulled the body clear of the water.

Mother and Father had happy days in Templeton Street. Mother takes up the story again:

Our first child Elizabeth, was born on a Saturday morning at 5 am. At the visiting hour, up came Bennie like a shot to see us, and was telling me, after seeing that everything was all right, that he would need to be hurrying back, as there was a regatta on. I had been waiting for this! My sister, who was with Ben, said, laughing: 'You're lucky to get him up at all. He has a taxi waiting out there to take him back.' He had been impatient to see us – visiting time couldn't come quickly enough – but once he saw everything was all right, he couldn't wait to get back to his Clyde.

It was lovely to come down Templeton Street and across the Green, with Elizabeth in her pram, to see her father. Most of our time was spent in the Green, going home in the middle of the day to make lunch, and again at tea-time.

66

Blood Clot

In the early part of 1935 and incident took place, which almost claimed Father's life in two ways. His number certainly hadn't come up that day! Firstly, the river did its utmost to take him, and then a blood clot in his leg, due to the great effort that had been needed to deny the river its prey, almost cut short this incredible career.

At 5.40 am there was a knock on the door at the house in Templeton Street, and when he opened it, a police officer was there to say: 'Bennie, there's a body jammed at the weir gates.' Even to this day, I hold a fear, a kind of dread, and certainly a lot of respect, for the river at the Tidal Weir. It is dangerous, even when it looks calm and serene, a very cruel part of the river, which shows little mercy to anything that gets in its grip. 'I'll come with you, Bennie, and give you a hand.' said the policeman.

Oblivious of what lay ahead, the two walked across the park to the boats and although the river was in flood and the tide was just on the turn, Father put the policeman in the stern of the boat and rowed downstream. I have often seen father work at the weir, or at some equally dangerous point, to recover an already dead body, and I never failed to marvel at the total dedication of a man who put himself in danger just to get a body, and alleviate the sorrow of relatives.

As they approached the weir, it was a typical situation: the north gate was down, the centre gate was half up, and the south gate was 6 or 7 feet out of the water. The policeman took the oars, and Father had him back the boat down to the north gate while he positioned himself, as usual, in the back of the boat, where he could lean over and tie the body up.

This he did in the usual way: a loop under both armpits. He tried to lift the body, which was on the girders at the back of the gate and must have been left there by the high tide, but it wouldn't budge.

A spot decision was made, and Father decided the only way to remove the body from the girders was from the down river side of the weir, so he threw the ropes over the gate, and took the oars again to row the boat round to the down river side. The way to get from the north gate upstream to the north gate downstream was through the open south gate. The river was in flood, and that, coupled with the tide running out, was making the river flow at one hell of a speed through the south gate. Father knew this was a tricky manoeuvre but he had done it so often, and, rowing hard against the water, he let his boat move out into the full current in front of the open gate and move slowly stern first downstream.

Suddenly, above the noise of the rushing water, Father heard the whir of mechanism and, looking up, was horrified to see the gate of the weir moving downwards at a rate that would coincide with them being directly under it, and would be their executioner. Father screamed at the weirman as loud as he could:

67

screamed with fear and fury as he tried to make himself heard above the noise of the machinery and the water. 'Get that gate up. UP, LIFT IT!' 'The tide's away,' shouted the weirman 'I can't let the water fall.' 'To hell with the tide, get the gate up!'

Another weirman ran onto the bridge, pushed the weirman out of the way, and slammed his hands on the 'lift' button. In the time that it took to shout to the weirman, and for the second weirman to lift the gate enough for the boat to pass under, Father rowed the boat, with the policeman sitting at the stern, helpless, at the mercy of fate and the skill of the man sweating in front of him, upstream inch by inch against the torrential water.

Every muscle strained; beads of sweat poured down; pressure, every bit of pressure that Father's superbly fit body could produce, plus the extra pressure found when one faces death face to face: the policeman said that he had never witnessed anything like it, and he certainly owed his life to Father's skill with the oars.

One has to have tried rowing into a heavy current in a small boat to realise how the current whips away the blade so fast, the swirling water tries to wrest the oar from its rowlock, and one has to see the weir at this state of tide and flood to realise the vortex, the undercurrent, the sheer volume of water that moves through the gates. I have seen motor boats not make it against this current, and have to anchor downstream to try again when the flood had lessened.

They now made their way downstream and across the river to pick up the ropes from the body. Meantime, the weirman had lowered the south gate and went to lower the centre gate. Anyone who knows anything about weirs will know that if the south and centre gates are put three-quarters down, with the north gate full down, the water will rise suddenly, and will pour over the north gate, so their troubles weren't over.

Father took the ropes which he had attached to the body, and, suddenly, water, debris and the body came flying through the air high above them as the water burst over the top of the gate, and the boat was half-filled and was swept by the current downstream, out of control, through the Albert Bridge. The body very nearly landed on top of them.

Father kept hold of the ropes from the body and, after he had taken control of the boat again, he was able to pull it in and fasten it up properly to finish the job. They landed the boat and the body at the ramp next to where the Molindinar enters the Clyde, carried it around the weir, and rowed home upstream.

The real extent of the pressure Father had applied to his lifeboat oars was only known the next morning when he lay in bed screaming with pain due to a blood clot caused by superhuman effort. He couldn't be moved to hospital in case the clot moved. It was touch and go. He lay there, with Mother laying cloths of almost boiling water on the leg. It is often said that God works in mysterious ways, and this was certainly true here – one of Mother's abilities was to withstand almost boiling water on her hands, and here was the opportunity for this talent to be used! This went on for eight days and nights before he was able to be moved to hospital. Although he was given a half tablet of morphine every two hours, half an hour later, he was screaming with pain again. For eight more days in hospital, he was given injections of morphine; his life was at stake if he moved too much.

Friends and relatives stood by the boats during these days, ready to work on Father's instructions if anything happened.

Fortunately, he made a good recovery, and was back to his work in no time. One strange thing was that Father held no grudge against the weirman!

The Queen Mary

A rare opportunity to combine work and pleasure followed, when Father was given the chance of a front stall view of a piece of Clydeside history: the launching of the *Queen Mary* in 1936.

He was asked by the Chief Constable of Renfrewshire to attend the *Queen Mary's* move down river for trials in the Firth of Clyde. Hundreds of the public were expected to flock to the Blythswood Estate opposite John Brown's Shipyard to see the boat going down river. This estate was very flat and could be flooded at high tide. A Clyde Trust launch the *Newark* was laid on for Father, and with two friends he went down river, from Renfrew Wharf to a point opposite Brown's dock.

Now these two friends were six feet plus: heavy Glasgow policemen who were off duty, and had asked Father if they could accompany him to watch the launching. So there they were, walking down the gangway onto the *Newark*, the two policemen (in plain clothes) followed by Father. One of the Clyde Trust officials, who had never met Father, came forward, hand outstretched, to the first policeman, and said, 'Good morning, Mr Parsonage,' 'no,' said the policeman 'we're only the assistants. He's the wee yin at the back.'

Father's rather diminutive stature always amazed people who, having heard of his exploits, expected a huge man.

The tug manoeuvred the *Queen Mary* down river, while the *Newark* kept an eye on the crowd.

When a large ship is being moved down river, it is done with the tide rising, so that if by any mishap the ship runs aground, the water will be rising and will float it again. So it was that some of the people who had flocked in their thousands to watch the *Queen* going down river, found themselves trapped by the fast-rising tide.

Opposite Bowling Harbour, Father spotted them. The Clyde Trust captain of the *Newark* couldn't take his boat to the people, who were up to their waist in rising water, because it was too shallow for his craft. They went into Bowling Harbour, where Father procured a rowing boat and took the people safely ashore. They then accompanied the 'Queen' down river before returning to Glasgow.

After the excitement and furore of the launching, work returned to, dare I say, 'normal', for on August 6th 1936 the headline in the *Evening Times* read:

THRILLING CLYDE RESCUE

'Man who went in to save his dog got into difficulties and was fortunately rescued by Mr Benjamin Parsonage of the Glasgow Humane Society who dived into the river fully clothed. While walking on the north bank of the river the man persuaded his dog, a small pomeranian, to go into the water. It seemed to him that the dog had got into difficulties and he then entered the water himself. The man who was unable to swim got out of his depth and was in serious danger when his plight was observed by Mr Parsonage who is stationed at the Glasgow Green. Without even taking time to divest himself of his outer clothing Parsonage dived into the water, swam out and caught hold of him.

Mr. Parsonage told a 'Times' man that he was none the worse of his experience. 'I was working in the boathouse near the bridge,' he said 'When I heard shouting, I ran out and saw a man disappearing beneath the surface of the water. I ran up the bank for about 200 yards and dived in. I had forgotten that my dungarees were loaded with heavy tools and the weight of these nearly pulled me under. I managed to get hold of the man who was exhausted and practically unconscious and then I fought my way towards the bank. It was a bit of a struggle as I was winded by running towards the spot before I dived in.'

Next day father was up at the canal, searching where clothing had been found on the towpath. This turned out to be a hoax. Later that month he rushed along the banking to where a small boy had fallen into the water, pulled him out, took him to his boatshed and let him dry his clothes, before sending him home with a promise to stay from the water in future.

Another incident in 1936 was reported in the *Glasgow Eastern Standard*, when a man was prevented by Father from throwing himself from the suspension bridge into the river. This man was fined a guinea or 14 days imprisonment for breach of the peace.

At least Christmas was spent in peace, but Boxing Day brought tragedy. Father was involved in a rather horrific case. Two men were working on the side of a ship in Fairfield's Dock, when a Carley Float broke away and came down the slides that were there to launch the float into the water. One of the men couldn't move out of the way fast enough, and he was decapitated by the steel girders of the float. His body landed on the deck where he had been working, but his head disappeared into the water, along with the float.

The Carley Float was lifted from the Clyde by crane, and the head was found jammed between the steel girders. It was removed and put into a rivet bag, which Father carried to the motor lorry he had used to bring his boat down, and had the driver take him to Govan Police Station, where it was put in the mortuary.

During 1936 a paper made this statement about Father's rescue work: 'Opportunity only comes to the minds that are prepared,' and of course Father always tried to be prepared.

Christmas Day 1936 may have been peaceful, but New Year's Day, 1937 was not to be so. At 12.30 am Father received word that an object like the body of a man had fallen from St Andrew's Suspension Bridge and disappeared. He rushed to the spot and made a search for several hours, without success.

Next day about 5 pm he recovered the body of the young man from the River Clyde, about 45 yards west of the bridge, near the south bank: someone, sadly, who had no wish to enter another year.

CHAPTER 6

Glasgow Green

At long last, in June 1937, the new house in Glasgow Green was completed, and the family moved in.

Dedication of Humane Society House

It was open door for everyone. All those who came were given a cup of tea and something to eat. Father had his first call out from his new home that same afternoon. Mother thought it was lovely for the children to have the Green to play on, but like everything else, it had its drawbacks. One of the disadvantages was crossing the Green to do her shopping, especially during the winter – no shops to run to if she found herself short of anything, so she just had to make sure she didn't.

The children had a sandpit and a swing in the garden, and family friends brought their children to play. When Elizabeth was three, Daddy made her a special pair of oars that her small hands could hold. He put a plank across the stern of a small rowing boat so that he could sit beside her and teach her to row. She learned before very long, and this small pair of oars was used in the same way for the rest of the family.

Messages did not come by telegram from the police station any more, the new house had a telephone installed.

The Telephone

What does a telephone ring mean to you? Is it just a noise, a nuisance, a means of chatting to your pals, a necessary modern evil? Do you leave if off the hook sometimes? Do you turn over and ignore it when it rings and you are in your bed for the night?

Once a telephone was installed in the house in the Green in June 1937, and an extension was run to the boathouse, the telephone bell became the signal to drop tools and sprint towards the source of the ringing.

It became a race to see if Father, at the boats, could answer it before Mother did in the house. Every second could mean the difference between life or death for someone in distress. 'Bennie, there's a man in the river at the weir.', 'Control here, Mr Parsonage, there's a woman in the river at the Kingston Bridge.', – 'Bennie, a man has jumped off the King's Bridge.', 'Land Rover coming to pick you up to take you to the County at Lanark, where there are people in danger of drowning from rising flood water.' The phone became a life-line.

As industry got noisier around our area, so the telephone engineers have had to put in larger bells, and now we have a klaxon, the noise of which matches the urgency of the rush to answer.

The seriousness of the mad scramble that commenced if the phone message was a 'call' was in direct contrast to the happy grin that broke over his weather-beaten face when Father heard a familiar voice, which told him that it was a 'non-business' call.

"After a successful rescue return to base at a leisurely pace."

Over the years there were various aids and improvements to the service Father offered the public, like the purchase of small outboard motors, which helped so often in carrying out searches. Father would use a 1 horse power Seagull, rather than 'waste' the time of a police officer having to row, or when they couldn't find a policeman who was able to row (an amazingly frequent happening, even in this city of Highland and Island policemen who were raised among fishing boats).

"A non-emergency departure!"

Over the years Father had many outboard motors and speedboats, but, with few exceptions, he did not use them for rescue work. He always said that if an engine did not start first pull, that could be the difference between life and death. His 'engine' (his rowing ability) always started first time and was very reliable. He would have needed to be going for a fair distance for it to be quicker by motor boat.

When he had to transport boats by land he used a lorry hired from a local firm, Brown's or Bryson's or he used the 'Black Marias'. Later two dispatch vans in the police garage at Helen Street used to come and take the boats by trailer, then, in the early 60s, came a police vehicle which opened up a large radius to Father's rescue work – the Land Rover – towbars in every Division – I have often wondered how many lives were saved per towbar! It must have been the most inexpensive device responsible for saving life in our business, a little invention that allowed Father to rescue people as far afield as Summerston Quay, Govan and Uddingston,

76

people hanging onto booms in Princes Dock, people stranded by rising water or floating just under the surface, prevented from sinking by some air trapped in their clothes. There are many instances where the immediate use of trailer saved a life, and we shall come to them later.

That first telephone ruled our life. You left the house to go to the boats, the phone rang and you made a spot judgement whether to run back to the house or to race for the boats. The phone could go at any time during the night, and you answered and reacted automatically before you were awake. I think I began to realise just what kind of reaction the telephone brought out in Father when, recently, while staying in a hotel in Nottingham when at the Holme Pierrepoint for an international rowing race the phone rang at 3 am and I had raced out in my pyjamas to answer it before I realised I wasn't in my own home! Still, Father was always at home, always on call. Not for him the pleasure of going anywhere to row in races, these were pleasures which I had at his expense.

The first ringing of a telephone was heard in the new house, and Ben Parsonage, Officer, resident again in Glasgow Green overlooking his beloved Clyde, was called out by the Glasgow police.

A newspaper carried the story:

FIRST CALL FROM HIS NEW QUARTERS TO DRAG CANAL FOR BOY VICTIM
Within two hours of his official opening of the new headquarters of the Glasgow Humane Society in Glasgow Green by the Secretary of State for Scotland yesterday, Mr. Benjamin Parsonage, who is in full charge there, was called with his rowing boat to drag the Forth and Clyde Canal, where it meets the Monkland Canal at Castle Street, near Garngad Road, yesterday evening. After only a short search, the body of a nine year old local boy was brought to the surface.

Death Customs

Over the years Father had to deal with people of many religions, and thus came into contact with varied customs and beliefs, like those he saw on January 5th 1938, when he was called to the George V Dock, where a crewman from a ship moored there had been drowned. After a short search the body of a man, who was Chinese, was brought to the surface.

The other Chinese crew members did no work, but just stood and watched the search until their friend's body was recovered. They gathered around the body, burned pieces of coloured paper and chanted, as their custom demanded.

The most common example was perhaps the Roman Catholic Priest who wished to come into the boat in order to give the last rites as soon as the body was recovered. On these occasions especially when it was a child, father would wet his handkerchief in the river, wash the child's face and tidy up the hair to make as presentable an appearance as possible before a relative or the clergy came along.

Father would often come home to ask Mother for a clean handkerchief, and she used to ask him what on earth he did with them. He would explain that he had used it to wash the face of somebody he had recovered from the water, then thrown it away. Mother soon learned not to enquire about the missing handkerchiefs, and to accept their loss as one of the many idiosyncrasies in Father's nature that transformed what could have been a very cold, hardened, 'just-another-job' attitude into the charming, shy, caring character that made him so highly thought of by people who came into contact with him.

The Hero Who Couldn't Swim

In March an official from Glasgow Corporation Baths Department called on Father regarding a man who had been given a job as a baths attendant. He had been awarded the Corporation Medal for Bravery when he jumped into the river and saved a man from drowning. He had gone to Plantation, where Arroll's were building the new quay, as he was out of work and looking for a job. He didn't get one, and was strolling dejectedly home along the waterside, when he saw a man in distress, jumped in and rescued him. As well as awarding the medal, the City Fathers decided to give him a job, and had sent him to Greenhead as a baths attendant.

The official had come to see Father about the fact that this man couldn't swim. How could they employ as a pond attendant someone who couldn't swim? Father said: 'Well, you'll just have to teach him. He got his medal for bravery, not for swimming!'

One day, a girl jumped off St Andrew's suspension bridge. She was fed up because she had lost her job and had decided to drown herself. Father rescued her before she could accomplish her grisly task. The doctor who answered Father's call for medical help sent her to Stobhill Hospital to be looked after. The matron in the hospital decided to help her get a job when she heard about her being out of work, so when she was well again she was taken on at the hospital: a happy ending!

During this time, Father maintained a boat and gear in a boathouse on the canal at Port Dundas, for use in the event of any accidents in the vicinity. Due to vandalism this could not be done today, and anyway, with trailers the boat travels with you.

1939 started as usual, with Father out on cases in various parts of the city. He even went back down behind the weir gates to recover the body of a man, putting himself in a similar dangerous position to that of a few years earlier when he almost lost his life there.

To this day I fear the weir. I treat it with great respect and awe. I am even wary of approaching the weir during tides and I would never consider coming up behind the weir at low tide to recover an already dead body.

I will always marvel at Father's careful yet carefree attitude, his superb ability in cases like this. I went with him a few time to the back of the weir to recover bodies, but I wasn't there of my own free will, but only because I knew I was in the care of the only person in whose hands I could feel safe. I remember Father's calming 'get-on-with-the-work' attitude making me almost forget my fears as I handed him the ropes to tie up a body. On one occasion, it could not be pulled away from the girders, so the ropes were thrown up onto the catwalk of the weir to the police officers, who then, under Father's directions, slowly pulled the body up, clear of the girders. Father pulled the body out so that it hung above the boat, then had the police lower it back into the water. We towed it to the bank, lifted it out, then it was taken to the city mortuary. Again the Clyde holds the secret of how this body entered the water.

Suicide Pact

At 6 am on Sunday May 28th 1939, a passerby discovered a bundle of clothes – a man's and a woman's – by the Clyde in the Bridgeton district of Glasgow. Two police officers hurried to the scene and, on searching the clothing, they found the grim evidence of a suicide pact – a sheet of notepaper bearing the message: 'We died together and wish to be interred together.'

Father was called in and, after a short search, he recovered the two bodies, lying close together in the river. While returning to his wharf at the suspension bridge with the two bodies, he also came across the body of a Glasgow man who had been missing since the previous Wednesday.

Police enquiries revealed that the dead woman's husband had been working away from home for some time. He had returned home on the previous Thursday to find his wife was out. She came home towards midnight, saying she had been at the cinema. The next day he saw her walking along Commerce Street with another man. The two men had started to argue, from words they had passed to blows, until bystanders separated them, and that was the last time the husband saw his wife or the other man alive.

Several young boys were involved in waterway incidents that summer of 1939.

In August Father was called by the police to the Albert Bridge where two boys were trapped on the girders underneath. As one newspaper said: 'They were rescued in dramatic fashion.'

A great crowd of people had gathered on the bridge and the bankings. Father raced to the scene by boat, taking a long ladder and rope with him. He had to approach from the river as there were no manholes through the deck of the bridge to allow any other access.

The boys were in the habit of going up onto the bridge when the water was away, climbing up the girders. There was a blank girder in the centre, and they would swing over this using a rope to the other side. The two trapped boys had done this, and the water had fallen away about 16 feet more than usual. They became too terrified of the height they were above the water to try to make their way back.

When he reached the north pier of the bridge, Father had a policeman hold the boat steady with a hook, he then put the ladder against the pier of the bridge and went up it. He just said to the policeman: 'See and hold the boat tight.' and up the ladder he went, yes, from a boat, with a rope over his shoulder!

He shouted to the boys to hold steady, he would lower them down, and crawled along the girders until he reached them. The boys were fourteen or fifteen years old and they just wouldn't let go or loose their grip, so Father fastened the rope around one of the boys, and put it over the girder to lower him down. He still wouldn't let go, and Father had to hit his hands to make him loosen his grip of fear: when he was swinging in mid-air on the rope he was screaming blue murder! He was lowered into the boat, and once his pal saw he was all right he didn't feel so bad, so he just let go and was lowered down easily.

Sometimes Mother and Father found themselves involved in unusual incidents, as happened on August 14th 1939 at 12.50 am when the doorbell rang. Father ran downstairs and on answering it was faced with a man covered in blood, a knife sticking out of his back. He was screaming his head off. Father brought him in and attended to him while Mother phoned the police and ambulance. He was removed to the Royal Infirmary.

Father and Mother dealt occasionally with accidents like that one, but the most common type of accident was like the one a few days later when a child of 3 crashed his tricycle on the brae outside and split his head. He was rushed into the house where Mother bathed his head while Father phoned the ambulance. He was removed to the Infirmary. The trike was kept until the boy's Father called for it a few days later.

Many injured persons were looked after in our house, ours being the only house in the area. People came to us to seek help or to report any injury, boys with broken arms, or severe injuries from having fallen on spikes, people fainting, epileptics, the old man who collapsed with a heart attack in the park but, unfortunately, could not be moved and passed away while Father was kneeling down beside him making him comfortable; children who had fallen off bikes, like the girl who did so and injured her eye. We couldn't get an ambulance so Father phoned the firm from whom he got the lorries to move his lifeboats, and took her to the Royal Infirmary in one of their cars.

Chapter 7

The War Years

August 28th 1939 was a day that Mother and Father long remembered. Father had just returned from taking the decomposed body of a man from the River Clyde when he had some unexpected visitors, strangers who were going to become part of everyone in Britain's life for many years to come, men whose business would change the face of Europe, men in uniform: officers of the Royal Air Force.

A Commanding Officer of the 947th Squadron RAF 'Balloon Barrage' with two other officers and three men asked that accommodation be given them, as the armed services were establishing bases all over the country. They were invited into the house where Mother gave them tea and cakes, and thus started a relationship which had its pleasing and its unhappy moments.

Troops moved into the boat clubs, and the Parsonage house was to be used as a medical base. Mother, Father and the children lived in two rooms and watched as their lovely, newly-built and decorated house was changed. Floors and walls were ripped up to install dental equipment, shelves were put up, beds arrived for the sick bay. One of the things that stuck out in Mother's mind was the pin-up pictures that the troops stuck to the wall with elastoplast.

Some of the troops arriving for examination would do things like tramp all over the garden. For every ordinary, good, honest member of the forces there seemed to be another who didn't care what he or she did. As Mother said, these years were a real education.

So it was that on 3rd September at 11 am, as Mother was preparing the RAF and family dinners, she was called into the living room and they all waited around the radio for the Prime Minister. Finally Neville Chamberlain's voice was heard, announcing that Britain and Germany were now at war. It had been expected. Mother and Father had known a few weeks earlier, but it was still a terrible shock when it arrived.

Anderson shelters were buried all over the Green; a small one for the family was buried in the garden and after the war we used it as a coal cellar.

Father, when he wasn't out on police work, doubled as an Air-Raid Precautions (ARP) Warden. When the sirens went, thousands of people came across the suspension bridge from the Gorbals and Hutchesontown, from Bridgeton, Calton and the Saltmarket into the Green to the shelters. The ARP Wardens had a difficult time getting the public to go right into the shelters as too many of them wanted to stand at the door and watch. Father used to go round from shelter to shelter during the air raids and collect baby's bottles, to take them to the house and heat the milk. He was also recovering bodies: it seemed, perhaps, that many men who remembered the horrors of the First World War had no wish to live through another and ended everything in the river.

The Humane Society House is white, and standing on its own as it does, it is quite a landmark. To the German bombers its position was even more important: the house stands at the first right-angled bend of the River Clyde. The Germans flew across country from Grangemouth, along the Forth and Clyde canal, turned upriver at Bowling and dropped their bombs. They then came on upriver to the first bend where, as I said, our house stands, and turned across country heading for home as the second wave of bombers came in.

Trenches were dug linking the Air Raid Shelters to each other, and Mother and Father were constantly giving medical aid to children who injured themselves falling into them.

One morning when Father went down to the boats he found the barges covered with shrapnel, and also several unexploded incendiary bombs lying on the banking. He gathered the incendiaries carefully, and carried them over to the Central Police Station.

Another day, when he returned from the canal having recovered the body of a man at 12.30 am, he told Mother that he had quite a job getting home as the blackout was now in force.

The shipyards and the docks were heavily guarded during this time, and movement around the river was very restricted. Troops had orders to shoot anything unusual moving on the river after dark in case it was enemy saboteurs, which made things difficult for Father at night. Unfortunately, one of the troops, a Royal Artillery man doing sentry duty on the south side of Finnieston Ferry, fell into the river during the blackout and was drowned. Father recovered the body the following morning.

Later that year, Father was dragging the river for a man at Berth 12 at Queen's Dock, when he picked up a large hawser – a steel rope from a ship. He told the person rowing the boat to do as usual, 'Row on out into the centre of the river and I'll drop this rope out of our road.' The rope was getting heavier and heavier, then Father saw the body of the man clinging to the rope – in his desperation to stop drowning, he must have caught hold of the rope and was now holding it in his death-grip. Father had great difficulty loosening the dead man's grip on the hawser.

Tragedy followed tragedy, and it was sad to see the following newspaper report:

GLASGOW NAVAL HERO DROWNED
One of the heroes of a recent sea fight between British and German ships has met his death in a Clyde port in dramatic circumstances. He was returning to his ship which was docked, when he is supposed to have fallen from the gangway into the water. This occurred on Friday night and a Petty Officer whose attention was attracted by screams saw the man struggling in the water and almost immediately disappearing.

New Year's Day

Owing to the blackout it was impossible to search for the body that night. However, the following morning Father recovered the body.

The first New Year's Day in wartime arrived, but they didn't have much time to think about this. Mother had a family of her own and the RAF to care for, and Father was kept busy at his work, as the following list for January 1940 shows:

Searched River Clyde at Stobcross Quay in heavy fog.
Recovered body of a man from the canal at White Bridge.
Search continued at Stobcross Quay.
Recovered body of a boy drowned in the Forth and Clyde canal while skating.
Searched canal at Firhill Basin.
Recovered body of a watchman from the Canal at South Speirs Wharf.
Recovered body of a watchman from the River Clyde at Yorkhill Basin.
Recovered body of a man from the Canal at Mid Wharf.
Recovered body of a man from the Canal at Berth 10 Maryhill.
Searched for man missing from Queen's Dock.
Searched for man missing from Barclay Curle's Scotstoun.
Recovered body of man at Stobcross Quay.
Searched for lightman missing at Shieldhall Wharf.
Searched for fireman missing from S.S. *Hektos*, Finland.
Searched for man at Barclay Curle's.
Recovered body of fireman from S.S. *Hektos*.
Searched for 4 days at Shieldhall before recovering body.
The man from Barclay Curle's was recovered some weeks later.)

This kind of recovery work went on constantly during the first years of the war, partly due to the increased shipping in the harbour, partly due to the fog, and to the people committing suicide because of the war. Bodies of Belgian, Canadian, Finnish, Norwegian, and many British seamen and soldiers were recovered.

The war brought many hardships. One day, a Glasgow newspaper heading read:

8 WEEKS' BABY, SISTER AND MOTHER SAVED

Constable Young, Glasgow Eastern Police, rescued an 8 week old baby. At the same time Benjamin Parsonage saved the baby's mother and three and a half year old sister who were also in the water. They are in Glasgow Royal Infirmary suffering from shock. Hundreds of people on the King's Bridge at Ballater Street saw the rescue. Constable Young was on the north bank at the time assisting Mr. Parsonage who was dragging the river for the body of a boy drowned on Saturday while canoeing. Mr Parsonage heard cries from the river bank that the mother and child were in the water. 'I pulled up the grappling irons' he told me 'rowed to the spot. I stood up in the boat as we came near the woman. I put my left hand down and caught her and at the same time reached over and gripped the girl with the other. I pulled them aboard and as I was doing this the crowd on the bank shouted "Get the baby." I looked over, saw something dark on the surface about 10 yards away, then there was a splash and the policeman was in the water rescuing the child.'

This woman had decided to end it all for herself, and her two children, when life became too difficult for her. Her husband was away in the Army and she was finding it difficult to cope. Her baby had started crying one night and she had put the light on in her house without first drawing the blackout curtains, and had therefore found herself in trouble with the police, and so took her dramatic action, throwing her family then herself into the river. But all ended well. When the police learned her story they arranged for her husband to come home on compassionate leave, and they flitted out of the district. Next day, Father recovered the body of the boy from the canoe incident.

As at the beginning of the year, so 1940 continued with almost constant work:

15th July Man drowned at Dalmarnock Bridge.
20th July Recovered body of man from River Clyde at Berth 15, Stobcross Quay at 12.15 a.m. during the blackout.
21st July Recovered body of a man from River Clyde near Millerfield Road.
22nd July Recovered body of the man at Dalmarnock Bridge.

The year was indeed a busy one. Father's boats had to be chained and anchored in midstream by Government order and when he wanted to build new lifeboats he had to apply in triplicate to the Ministry of Defence.

My sister Ann was born on February 15th 1941, while the Air Force were still in the house. There was great excitement that night. We always tell her that not only her Father came in to see her, but in trooped half a dozen airmen. Ann was christened in the Central Church of Scotland in Charlotte Street. The minister had just finished the christening when there were loud noises that many of you, unfortunately, will remember vividly: the noise of explosions nearby and of air raid sirens sounding.

Mother remembered it well. The minister put his hands up and said, 'Don't panic. If anyone wants to leave they may do so, but we shall continue and finish the service.' When they came out to walk home across the Green, they heard the noise of aeroplanes, and looking up, witnessed a 'dog fight' between a British fighter and a German bomber. The bomber was brought down in Kilsyth.

One night a message was received that a soldier and the lorry he was driving were reported missing in George V Dock. Father was asked to make a search, and was concentrating on the left-hand corner of the dock when he came across an obstruction that he could not move. He asked that a Clyde Navigation Trust Diver search the spot; the diver went down and found the soldier and the lorry all right, but next to the lorry was an unexploded German bomb. Had the grappling irons touched the bomb there would have been little left of the boat or the quayside! The Army took over the recovery work.

On the evening of May 5th Father was called to the River Clyde at Shore Street. Helped by the police, he was in the process of lifting the body up the banking when suddenly the air raid sirens sounded. As both Father and the police had duties to perform during these raids, the body was put back into the river and fastened with a rope to a post on the banking.

At 6 am the following morning, he returned to Shore Street to finish the recovery work. After fastening the body of the man to his boat just upstream of Shore Street, he discovered the body of another man. This he also fastened to his boat and towed the two bodies downstream to the wharf at the Green. On bringing the boat alongside the barge, the police were waiting to tell him that there was the body of a man caught at the south gate of the Tidal Weir.

Tying the two bodies to the barge, he went down to the south gate and fastened up the man's body. He rowed across the river to come up the north bank and discovered the body of a man at the north gate; this also was tied up and again two bodies were rowed, this time upstream, to the wharf.

The four bodies were lifted onto the barge and then removed by the police to the City Mortuary. With Father having taken four bodies from the river that day, there was a rumour going around that they were the bodies of German paratroops.

A lot of children, sadly, were drowned during 1941, possibly because so many parents were away from home. On Christmas Day Father recovered the body of an 11-year-old boy from the River Cart; this boy had been given a Christmas present of a football, which accidentally landed in the river. He had taken off all his clothes, entered the water to try to retrieve it and drowned.

One day Father was called to the Forth and Clyde Canal at Whitbread Brewery, opposite the canal workshops, where a van had been driven into the canal. A diver from Falkirk was searching for the man but couldn't find him. Father managed to locate the van, and the diver went down the ropes but found no one in it. From the diver's description of how the van was lying Father worked out where he thought the man had gone, and after a few minutes search he recovered the body. During this search the crowds packed the towpath so tightly that a woman was pushed, accidentally, into the canal and Father had to rush along in his boat and rescue her.

Spring came, and the cold weather started to disappear, but there was no let-up in the drowning accidents. On April 13th Father was called to George V Dock to recover the body of a man floating there. He discovered that there were two puncture wounds in his left breast and so the CID were sent for. A newspaper carried a report:

MAN WITH WOUNDS DIED FROM DROWNING
After examination of the Doctor's report of the post-mortem made on the body of a man, with wounds on the chest, that was taken from the River Clyde on

Monday, the detectives who are in charge of the investigations are satisfied that the man died from drowning. It was first suspected that the wounds had been inflicted before the man entered the water. But later it was thought he received the wounds in the water caused by some obstruction striking him. His body was recovered by Ben Parsonage near King George V Bridge, Glasgow, and apparently had been in the water for two or three weeks.

Among the many cases Father was involved in was one when he took the body of an 8-year-old girl from the emergency water tank at Kintyre Street and some days later the body of a 4-year-old boy from a similar tank in Savoy Street. When it was reported that the bodies of children had been recovered from emergency water tanks, the Lord Provost of Rutherglen suggested that additional protection should be given and stated that, in Rutherglen, the tanks were being covered over solidly, mostly with wood.

Rosie

One day Father went out between 7 and 8 am to see his boats. When he came in, he told Mother that he was watching a woman who was hanging about; Father always was suspicious of anyone hanging about. The police phoned and asked Father to go out and search the canal for a boy who had been drowned. He wasn't sure of going as he was not happy about this woman, but Mother said that she would keep an eye on her. Father recovered the body of the boy and returned home. The woman was still hanging around but, while that was suspicious to Father, it wasn't a crime so he went into the house for his dinner.

He was sitting at the table in the kitchen with Mother, eating his dinner when the door bell rang. Father always sat at the table seat nearest the door for speedy answering, and this day it proved a useful move. The door opened and a man shouted, 'Bennie, there's a woman in the river downstream of the boats.' Father dropped his fork and sprinted down the garden path, down the brae, jumped the fence, down the banking and dived into the water, caught hold of the woman and pulled her to the bank. Some men helped them up the bank to the Humane Society House. Mother took charge of the woman. Father said she had been wearing a big black straw hat with a rose in it, and she was immediately nicknamed 'Rosie'.

'Rosie' had a black lace dress clinging to her, and when mother removed it, she discovered that she was wearing nothing else. She was made comfortable until the arrival of an ambulance. Mother was of the opinion that this woman had no intention of drowning herself, but was only looking for a bit of attention and somewhere to stay, and that she deliberately waited till Father came home to jump in, hoping and trusting that she would be rescued.

In September Father was asked to search the Monkland Canal for a woman who had murdered her two children while temporarily insane. He searched for three days before the woman turned up alive in Ayrshire. While he was searching for this woman, two policemen came along the canal towpath. They said that they were searching for a man supposed to have jumped into the canal. Father joined the search and recovered the body.

More examples of Father's continuous work and of his amazing capacity for rowing are as follows:

November 4th 1942. Rowed down river to Springfield Quay and recovered the body of a man from Port Gordon at Berth 37.

Rowed to Meadowside and at No. 3 Berth recovered the body of a man who had fallen from the S.S. *Blyktor.*

Continued down river to King George V Dock and searched for two men who were reported missing the previous night when thick fog lay over the harbour.

November 5th. Recovered the body of a ship's engineer at Berth 9 King George V Dock, one of the missing men.

Left the dock at about 10.30 a.m. and rowed to Rothesay Dock, Clydebank to make a search for a soldier who had gone missing during the previous day again in heavy fog.

November 6th. Searched for soldier.

November 7th. Searched for soldier at Rothesay Dock. Rowed upriver to the King George V Dock and after several hours search recovered the body of the second man at Berth 5. Left the dock and rowed upstream to the River Kelvin at Henderson's Shipyard to search for a man who went missing in thick fog.

Searched from this day to 13th November without success. This man's body was found several weeks later as was the body of the soldier in Rothesay Dock.

Another Christmas and New Year, and still tragedy in the water. The year was only a few days old when word was brought to the Parsonage house that part of a WAAF uniform had been found on the canal bank near to Oakbank Hospital. Father arranged a lorry to take his boat to the spot and after a short search he recovered the body of a young woman about half a mile away. As he rowed back along the canal to where there was access by road he came across the body of a man. Both bodies were removed to the mortuary.

People kept falling in during the blackouts or the thick Glasgow fogs. In later years, that is one thing that Father was so glad was a thing of the past: the real Glasgow pea-souper.

Quarries were in abundance around Glasgow at this time and these even more than the canal, which was still at least in partial use, were the main danger areas for children playing on rafts, for it was here that the material for building rafts was to be found, without the presence of adults to chase them away. Most of these quarries have disappeared from the landscape: Foxley Quarry, Wee Kenmuir (a quarry hole abut 75 yards wide at Kenmure), Bishopbriggs Quarry, Colston Quarry, Lightburn Quarry, Slag Pond at Dixon's Pit, White Rock Quarry, the quarry at Shettleston Piggery, the quarry hole at Barmulloch Farm, the disused pool near the Royston Brick Works, another quarry at Sandyhills Golf Course, the quarry at the Stepps Road and many more unnamed holes.

Another reason for many drownings during these years was that people, mostly boys, went bathing in the River Clyde and the canals. Glasgow now has many swimming pools and there is no reason for anyone to swim in the river or canals, it is just foolhardy. Thankfully, parents and youngsters seem to have acquired more sense, and that, coupled with the vigilance and teaching of people like Father, means that seldom now does anyone put their life in danger by attempting to swim in these places.

The months passed, with people rescued, bodies recovered, hours spent in the air raid shelters, as the west of Scotland was bombed. One night the remains of the old Infirmary at the foot of Charlotte Street received a direct hit and, as Mother sat with her children in the shelter, the bang seemed so near that she remembers thinking 'Well, that's the house gone, but at least we're safe and well.' Father? Well, he was around somewhere with the ARP.

On October 15th 1943, with Father's work continuing in the midst of war, I was born. Father and Mother got on well with the airmen billeted in the house, and one of them, known only as 'Archie', who had been moved away just before I was born, wrote me the following letter:

Dear George,
Welcome to this world of ours such as it is a present, it is most unfortunate that you could not have been born under the happier conditions of peace-time, however it will not I'm sure be very long before victory is ours and you will know a better place to spend a long and happy life. I must apologise for not being present at your christening old chap but circumstances would not permit, I will though if it is at all possible be in Glasgow for your first birthday and with your permission assist you in blowing out the candles on your cake. Again old chap, I wish you every success and happiness in the coming year.

Yours very sincerely, Archie.

We never heard from him again.

At 6 am one morning in 1944 the doorbell rang, and when Father opened the door a man told him that he had stood at the foot of Waddell Street and watched what he thought was a boy swimming about the river who had suddenly disappeared near the north side. Father ran down the north bank, and at a point about 150 yards west of the Glasgow Humane Society's house he found a woman's coat. On searching further with a boat he recovered the body of a woman. It was assumed that she had fallen down the banking.

The following week the doorbell rang again, and when Father opened the door, two Canadian Seamen and a girl said they had seen a girl disappear in the River Clyde near to the Printers' Clubhouse. He rushed to the lifeboat and rowed upstream, when suddenly his oar struck something under the surface. Reaching under the water, he caught hold of a woman, lifted her into the boat and applied artificial respiration. He continued resuscitation at the wharf until the arrival of the ambulance and the police. On arrival at the Infirmary she was found to be dead. She had been too long in the water before the alarm was raised.

At noon the same day Father recovered the body of a man from the river at the Suspension Bridge. The body had only been in the water for about twelve hours.

A few days later, a young woman was looking over the parapet of the Suspension Bridge, lost her balance, and fell into the river close to the bank. Father rushed to the spot but could do nothing as the woman had landed in about four feet of water and had broken her neck.

That evening around 11.30 pm Father was just settling down for the evening when the doorbell rang and he was informed that there was a man in the river near Waddell Street, screaming for help. The man had taken too much to drink, and had boasted to his pals that he could swim the Clyde.

Father rushed for a lifeboat and rowed to the spot as fast as he could. The man was in real trouble and kept disappearing and re-appearing. When Father got alongside him he had sunk way down below the surface, and he had to lean right over the boat and down into the water to catch hold of him. He lifted him into the boat and applied artificial respiration until he regained consciousness.

The man was taken to the medical room in our house and put to bed until the arrival of the ambulance. He had been so near to death that he was detained in hospital for three days, then handed over to the police. Father sent two men who knew him to get his wife and, while he was in the medical room, she arrived. She said 'Whit did ye risk yer life for that bugger? You should have let him drown.' Two or three weeks later, Mother was at the window and shouted downstairs 'Hey Bennie, come and see this!' When he looked out the window, there, walking up the brae, was the rescued man and his wife arm-in-arm like young love!

Boat building

As I said earlier, Father had to apply to the Government for permission and material to build boats. Some of the letters that passed between Father and the Admiralty at that time make interesting reading, because, as Bennie Parsonage found out, it required the same form-filling whether you were building a small rowing boat or a battleship!

In April a girl fell from St Andrew's Suspension Bridge. Father jumped into his boat and rescued her. He took her to the house where she was put to bed and looked after by Mother until the arrival of an ambulance to take her to the Royal Infirmary, where she recovered. My sister Ann, being very young at this time, saw Father carrying the girl into the house. She thought the girl was a friend whom she knew quite well. So sure was she in her mind of this that for years after she could not be convinced that it had not been this girl.

In the later years of the war, Father and Mother went out for the evening. Some of Father's friends said, 'Go on Bennie, take Sadie across to the 'Bees' tonight. We'll watch the boats and let you know if the police want you – surely things will be all right for a few hours.' So off they went to the 'Bees' – the Wellington Palace picture hall, in Commercial Street just across the river. They were enjoying themselves, watching the picture, with their coats on their knees, and a box of chocolates, when there was an interruption in the film – up on the screen was flashed the message: 'Will Ben Parsonage please go to the Manager's office.' The manager told him that the police needed him. Father and Mother hurried back across the bridge: Father went down to the boats and rowed downstream to recover the body of a woman from the river.

91

FORM M.S.2.

LICENCE No. 935

The Restriction of Construction of Ships Order, 1940, dated January 31st, 1940, made under Regulation 55 of the Defence (General) Regulations, 1939.

LICENCE TO BUILD A SHIP

In pursuance of Article 1 of the Restriction of Construction of Ships Order 1940, the Admiralty hereby authorise (subject to compliance with the conditions mentioned below) the construction by Benjamin Parsonage Esq.

(hereinafter called the Builder)

to the order of Glasgow Humane Society

of the ship (known as Yard No. -) of which particulars are given overleaf.

CONDITIONS.

1. The hull and machinery of the ship shall, unless the Admiralty at any time direct otherwise, be constructed in strict accordance with the hull and machinery specifications and general arrangement plan approved by the Admiralty.

2. The Builder shall carry out and conform to any alterations in the specifications and plans which the Admiralty may whether on the grant of this licence or at any other time direct in writing to be carried out.

3. The keel of the ship shall be laid by the 30th day of September, 19 44 or by such later date as may be endorsed hereon or directed in writing by the Admiralty and construction shall proceed with all despatch with a view to delivery of the ship on about 19 , or such later date as may be endorsed or directed as aforesaid.

4. This licence is not transferable and may be revoked by the Admiralty at any time.

5. Immediately on any failure to comply with any of the above conditions this licence shall automatically determine.

NOTE—The execution after the revocation or determination of the licence of any work for or in respect of the ship will be an offence against Regulation 55 of the Defence (General) Regulations, 1939.

Signed by authority of the Admiralty this 27th day of June, 19 44.

92

CHAPTER 8

A Troubled Peace

The war finished, though times were still hard with food rationing and shortages, and things were gradually settling down, boat hiring was getting back to normal, more of the rowing club members were coming back from the war, and the river was getting busier again.

Less people wanted to drown themselves as they weren't so frightened of the war now, or they had managed to come to terms with the fact that life could go on even without the loved ones they had lost. There were still an awful lot of accidents in the harbour as there was more shipping here than I, or most of you, will ever see again. Every berth was occupied at this time: even double-berthing was commonplace.

The tidal weir once again was the setting for a very dangerous recovery of a body. One day Father received a call from the weirman that there was a body lying over the bottom girder of the gate on the downside. Father went down in his boat taking a 10-foot ladder with him. He manoeuvred the boat alongside the gate and carefully propped the ladder so that it sat on the bottom ledge where he could climb down it. I shiver to think of this, even as I write. If you don't feel a shiver running up and down your spine too, then take a walk down to the Green and have a look at the weir at low tide. It's easy enough to write, 'Climb down the ladder and stand on the bottom ledge and tie the body up with a rope under each arm, then climb back up to the boat carrying the ropes.' Every word of that statement spells danger, and that's exactly what Father did. He then threw a rope up to the weirman and the police 30 feet above him. The body was then lifted up until it hung high enough to enable Father to swing it upstream to the gate and lower it into the water beside the boat. He rowed upstream to the wharf and the body was removed to the mortuary.

There then followed a search in the Clyde for a lost boy. The *Evening News* of Wednesday July 17th 1946 reported:

> The body of a 10 year old boy was recovered from the Clyde this afternoon by Mr. Benjamin Parsonage. With his seven year old brother and a friend they had climbed on to the girders of the Central Station Railway Bridge last night to look for pigeon's nests. The boy's father waited by the riverside as Mr. Parsonage

resumed dragging, his younger son by his side still red eyed, cried a little and wanted to go home. At one point he suddenly looked up to the bridge 'Look' he said pointing to one of the hundreds of pigeons which nest there 'There's my brother's lady white up there!'

I managed to lay my hands on a report that Father had drawn up for the police:

BRIDGE TRAGEDY

Angus points out to Mr Benjamin Parsonage, of the Royal Humane Society, the spot where his brother fell into the Clyde from the girders of the bridge outside the Central Station last night.

16.7.46
I arrived at the Bridge Wharf at the Glasgow Central Railway Bridge at 1 am on the 16th to search for a boy who had fallen from the bridge and was drowned, while bird watching.
I searched all night until 8 am on the 17th at a point 17 yards from the north bank pointed out to me by the police. I satisfied myself that the boy was not there and came to the conclusion that there was something wrong with the information supplied. Suspended operations for the meantime and went for my breakfast. At 9 am I phoned the Central Enquiry to find their information the same as mine. I asked the sergeant if he could possibly get the brother of the boy who had been present at the time of the accident to come and verify the information.
Arranged to meet at 10 am. At 10.45 am the boy and I went up on the the catwalk of the bridge and went along the bridge to the place where the boy said his brother had fallen in. This spot was right on the other side of the river from which I had searched previously. On resuming operations I recovered the boy's body at 11.20 am.

A few days later, in the early afternoon, an elderly lady jumped from St Andrew's Suspension Bridge into the River Clyde. Father raced out in his boat and lifted the woman, who was all of 15 stone, into the boat and raced back to the landing stage. With the help of another man, the woman was taken to the house, where Mother stripped and dried her and put her to bed. Mother gave her tea and biscuits. She was upset because nobody wanted her, and she had lost her handbag and pension book (sunk in the river). She asked could she not stay where she was and live with Mother and Father, as they were the only people who had cared what had happened to her for years, but she had to be removed to hospital, and on the arrival of the ambulance she was taken there. Fortunately,

94

the woman made a good recovery and her relatives took a renewed interest in her welfare. Another sad case had a happy ending.

It was around this time that Father recovered the body of a man from the River Clyde at Erskine. A few days late he received this letter:

THE PRINCESS LOUISE SCOTTISH HOSPITAL FOR MAIMED AND LIMBLESS SAILORS AND SOLDIERS

TEL NO BISHOPTON 40
TELEGRAMS ERSKINE BISHOPTON

ERSKINE
BISHOPTON.
RENFREWSHIRE

Physician Superintendent–
COL.T. H. SCOTT. D.S.O. M.C. M.B.

Ref. Misc./P/11/45.

26th November, 1945.

Dear Sir,

On behalf of Erskine Hospital, I would like to thank you very much indeed for the help you gave us yesterday in recovering the body of J.B.S. Hutcheson from the Clyde.

Joe had been a patient here for a long time and was a gentle, likeable man with whom everybody got on well.

He was however not very sure on his feet and so never walked outside the grounds. In summer he was in the habit of going down to the water's edge and I fear that with walking in the dark last Monday he must have fallen in and the rising tide caught him.

Will you please accept the enclosed as a small remembrance of Joe.

With renewed thanks for your help.

Yours faithfully,

Physician Superintendent.

Col. T.H. Scott, D.S.O. M.O. S.C. M.B.,
Physician and Superintendent,
Erskine Home,
Bishopton,
Renfrewshire.

To which Father replied:

```
                                        28th November 45.

    Dear Sir,

                    J.B.S Hutchison - deceased.

            I have to acknowledge receipt of your registered
    letter, dated 26th instant, in which was enclosed the sum of
    Two Pounds, (£2).

            I very much appreciate your very fine gesture in
    forwarding me this monetary gift but I consider what I did
    in recovering the body of the deceased J.B.S. Hutchison from
    the River Clyde, only part of my daily work, and I would
    therefore be very pleased, if you would accept the Two
    Pounds I return herewith, with the request that it be
    utilised for the benefit of your most worthy and deserving
    ex. soldiers Home.


                                        Yours truly,


    Mr. Benjamin Parsonage,
    Glasgow Humane Society,
    Glasgow Green,
    GLASGOW, C.5.
```

After the war many children were without parents to look after them many having been killed in action, or in hospital. Also, many children were allowed out to play more them. As a result, a lot of children drowned in Glasgow waterways. The following is a list of some of the drowning accidents that occurred during the winter of 1946/47 and it gives some idea of the tragic incidents that Father was involved in.

A Troubled Peace

Boy of 5 recovered from River Cart.
Boy of 9 recovered from Forth and Clyde Canal.
Boy of 4 recovered from Monkland Canal.
Boy of 12 recovered from Forth and Clyde Canal.
Boy of 5 saved. River Clyde.
Boy of 13 recovered from River Clyde, Cambuslang.
Boy of 5 saved. River Clyde.
Boy of 5 recovered from Forth and Clyde Canal.
Boy of 7 saved. River Clyde.
Boy of 3 recovered from River Cart.
Boy of 4 recovered from Forth and Clyde Canal.

Mother well remembered these days; Father would be away searching some waterway when the phone would ring and the police would tell her that his services were required elsewhere. Mother would sit at our hall window, watching for Father returning home with his boat on the lorry. She would hang out the window and shout 'Bennie! Don't let the lorry go; you're wanted at the canal in Maryhill!' or some other locus.

In March 1947 he was called to the River Cart. Govan Police were investigating the disappearance of a 6-year-old boy whose clothes were found lying on the bank of the river. The boy was last seen when he left home for school. Later his clothes and schoolbag were found on the river bank within a short distance of his home. Father began dragging operations in a number of deep holes near the spot where the boy's clothes were found. The River Cart was in spate. The Clyde was in heavy spate too, and it was in these very dangerous conditions that Father rescued a man downstream of the suspension bridge outside the house. He recovered the body of the boy in the Cart about three weeks later.

Around this time, Father recovered the body of a man who had fallen from the SS *Ardochy* moored at Custom House Quay. It's interesting to note that Custom House Quay was the wharf for gravel and sand unloading and the *Carrick* was moored just east of Jamaica Bridge.

New Year came and work continued. We were now at peace; there were no blackouts, or troops with guns at the ready to worry about. The rowing clubs were back to normal, and regattas were again commonplace.

In April Father was in his boat following a skiff race when, coming round the final bend, he saw a four-oared boat lying upside down in the water with five members of the Stirling Amateur Swimming and Boating Club hanging on to it. He rushed to their aid in his lifeboat, powered by a newly purchased 'Seagull' outboard. My older sister, Elizabeth, was in the boat with Father. He lifted the five into his boat and took them to the steps of the clubhouse. The cox boy was only worried about the loss of a sandshoe, so Father went out and searched around the debris on the river until he found the shoe. Onlookers say that Father was given the biggest cheer of the day when he returned the shoe to the boy!

Another child drowning tragedy was reported on Wednesday August 2nd.

ROPE DESCENT TO RECOVER BODY

A rowing boat had to be lowered by ropes down the steep face of a dangerous pool in the River Clyde near Lanark at the weekend in order that the body of a 9 year old boy who had been drowned there might be recovered. Mr. Benjamin Parsonage lowered himself down the dangerous rocks from high above the water. After hours of dragging the pool he recovered the body. Mr. Parsonage and his boat travelled by road from Glasgow after all attempts to recover the boy's body had failed.

This rock face is over 120 feet high. According to witnesses, they could not believe their eyes as they watched Father pay out the rope foot by foot as he lowered himself and the boat down the rock. After he recovered the boy's body, he climbed back up the rope carrying the boy in his arms.

One day when Father was taking his customary row downstream in the direction of the tidal weir he noticed a coat lying on the bank at a point facing Nelson's Column on the north bank. Father was always suspicious of things like this; he started to search around the area and found the body of a man which had only been in the water a few hours.

Frequently Father spotted something suspicious like this: one time he noticed marks in the long grass on the banking next to the suspension bridge and, on investigation, found the body of a man lying in shallow water. A similar incident occurred not long before his death, when a coat floating downstream caused him to search upriver, where he found the body of a woman.

On May 16th 1949 Father was called to a point on the River Clyde between the Clyde Iron Works and Tollcross Sewage Works, where a boy of ten was drowned when he was swept off his feet while trying to ford the river from the north bank to an island. The river runs very fast at this point. He recovered the boy's body after three days of searching.

Swimming the Clyde

Swimming the Clyde is daft, but swimming the Clyde as a definite means of escape to the other side is another matter. Like the case that occurred on 24th September 1973. Somewhere in Glasgow there are three youths who know the true story of what happened that day and would probably be in hysterical laughter about it. About 10.45 pm, Father received a call from the Eastern Police requesting that he attend with the boat and lamps at the sewage works. Father and I proceeded there immediately, and were told that three youths had been chased, after an assault and robbery in Springfield Road, to the river, and were last seen diving into the heavy bushes on the riverbank.

We searched along the water's edge. Police dogs searched the long grass; the police support unit searched all along the towpath; and the Rutherglen police kept vigilance on the south side. The youths were never caught; they must have entered the water and swam up or downstream to escape. As I say, only they know.

One youth was not so lucky. Father received a call at 10.30 pm from Craigie Street Police Office asking if he would go to Boggleshole Ford, where there had been a youth drowned. Father went by Land Rover to the Clydebridge Steel Works, where the boat was launched. Three boys had tried to swim the river to escape from a gang. Two made it but one had drowned. While they were in the water, the gang threw stones at them. Father recovered the body after about 20 minutes.

Many people get drunk, take a 'daft' turn and try to swim the river. Some are lucky and get out again; some don't make it. In 1953 Father was told that a man was in the River Clyde near to the Printers' Boathouse. He raced upriver and took the man into his boat and returned with him to the wharf. In the house, he stripped and dried him and put him to bed. His excuse for being in the water was one that we have heard many times: that he wanted to swim the river.

August 12th 1973 is a day that I remember well. It may have been the 'glorious twelfth' for some, but for Father it was another day when he was saved by his incredibly quick reflexes.

About 10 pm we received word that there was a man in the river Clyde at the Jamaica Bridge. We rushed the trailer out just in time to meet the Land Rover, hitched the trailer and jumped into the back of the vehicle. It sped off, lights flashing, to the ramp at where the police patrol boat used to be below the railway bridge. The boat was launched and I rowed as fast as I could to where the young man was hanging onto a lifebelt. Father sat on his plank at the back of the boat getting his ropes and other equipment ready. I swung the stern around and carefully backed down so that Father could catch hold of the man who was at this time lying prone in the water.

Father leaned over the stern to lift him into the boat, when suddenly the limp figure tried to grab hold of him and pull him into the water. Father kept out of the way of the flailing hands and the biting teeth. He caught hold of one arm. Anyone who has had the 'misfortune' of Father catching hold of them will know his grip is like iron. Father fastened a rope round the man's arm and, holding the man by the rope, he tried to talk some sense into him so he could lift him into the boat. Every time he did so, the man just tried to pull him into the water, shouting and swearing one minute, then faking unconsciousness the next to try to catch Father unawares.

99

When all normal means of rescue were obviously failing, Father caught hold of the youth by the hair. The youth tried to climb into the boat to fight, but Father had a good hold of him and pushed him back into the water. 'So, you want to drown do you?' said Father and promptly shoved his head under the water and held him there for a few minutes before bringing him up to ask again, 'Had enough?' Snarling teeth and an attempted bite were the answer, so Father shoved him under again to subdue him, and managed to get another rope round him. Thus tied up, he couldn't be lifted into the boat, so he was towed to the wharf with Father sorting out the spasmodic attempts that were made to attack him. The ropes were thrown up to the police and the man, still struggling violently, was lifted up on to the quay wall. It took half a dozen or more policemen to hold him and handcuff him. He was removed to the Royal Infirmary.

A similar incident occurred on August 6th 1975 almost two years later. About 8.15 pm I was down at the wharf when I was approached by a man who asked how he could get to the skyscrapers on the other side of the bridge. I told him to go across the bridge and down the opposite banking. He then started acting very strange, wanting to play children's games, and then he suggested swimming the river. I realised that this man was, at least temporarily, insane and I tried to get him through our gate into the Park and away from the river, but without success. He rushed off, skipping and dancing, down the bank, so I raced to the telephone, dialled 999, then contacted Father on the extension.

Father ran down from the house and joined me in time to see the man wade out into the water, climb onto one of our pontoon barges, run along the barge, then dive into the river and swim towards the opposite bank. We jumped into the lifeboat and double-sculled to where the man was swimming diagonally downstream. Father pulled his oars in and moved to the stern of the boat as I manoeuvred it close to the swimmer. He half swam, half waded through the weeds, ducking out of our way every time Father went to catch him. 'Stay close, stay close' Father shouted at me, 'Keep as close to him as you can, he's getting tired.' Sure enough, suddenly Father lunged over the side of the boat, arms down into the water to his shoulder blades, and just caught hold of the man, who had suddenly sunk in the weeds.

We lifted the man into the boat, where Father applied artificial respiration and brought him round. Police cars had arrived by this time, lights flashing and sirens blaring, and I was pleased to see policemen, hats in hands, sprinting across the suspension bridge and along the banks to our aid. It's good to know that they're there if you need them; they were going like the clappers, because they thought Father was in trouble. Our resuscitator had been brought to the wharf in case we needed it, but Father had brought the man round in his own way. It took many policemen to help this man, who seemed completely terrified now, into the police van. Father had to be forced to go to the Royal Infirmary, as we discovered that the man had given him a nasty bite on the hand when he had reached down into

Next day Father launched his boat at the old pulp mill, and went down river to where the cow was lying. He fastened it up and tried to pull it to the bank, but the water was too shallow. The work was very dangerous because of the current. The bullock could not be moved, so Father tied it up to stakes driven into the bank, where it stayed until proper arrangements could be made to remove it.

One day the klaxon blared and Father answered the phone to a man from the Department of the Environment, who asked Father if he could do something about the body of a donkey in the Clyde, near Rutherglen Motor Boat Club. Father phoned the Rutherglen police, as he would need help to lift the body onto the bank, and of course the police would have to arrange for its disposal. It was very hot weather and a carcass couldn't be left out of the water for any time. The Rutherglen police phoned back to say that the undertakers wouldn't do anything, that it was the Cleansing's job, and they were trying to arrange for them to attend.

Father was already away upriver to the scene when I received a call, this time from the Eastern police. It seems that the Rutherglen police had phoned the Eastern police to inform them that the body of a donkey in the river was now in *their* territory, having floated downstream.

The policemen in the Eastern asked me, 'Have you any idea how this donkey got in the river?' I couldn't resist it; I said 'It fell on its ass and slid down the bray into the river!'

I told the Eastern that Father was upriver but could do nothing till the arrival of the Cleansing to remove the body. The Eastern failed to get the Cleansing to attend immediately, and by this time the donkey had floated into Central Division and down to the weir.

Father finally contacted the Central and had them arrange for the Clyde Trust to come upriver and remove the donkey.

One day we received a call that there was an object that could be a body jammed at the foot of the dam at Kelvingrove Park. Father went to the Kelvin and found the body of a pig, which could not float away because of the back flow of water at the bottom of the dam. He pulled the pig clear of the dam and it went sailing off down the Kelvin. On seeing what it was, the large crowd which had gathered disappeared.

One Saturday afternoon the buoys had been laid and the stakeboats moored for the afternoon regatta when, around the bend above the start of the race, came a large object floating on the surface – a large bull. Father tried to steer it clear of the buoy ropes, shouting for the club members to move the buoy ropes from the banks, but they were too slow and the bull caught firmly on one of the ropes. The regatta had to be held up, and then rowed without the inside lane, while the difficult work of moving the heavy carcass into deep water and freeing it from the ropes took place.

As I have said, there have been many such incidents and, at times, they can be light-hearted digressions from the more serious work.

CHAPTER 10

Into the Fifties

On December 9th 1949 newspapers reported:

MYSTERY OF CAR IN CLYDE. Police and Mr Ben Parsonage early this morning searched the wreckage of a grey saloon car found late last night almost completely submerged in the River Clyde 100 yards upstream from Dalmarnock Bridge. By torchlight police traced the tracks of the car which had plunged over a 40 foot drop into the fast flowing river. They found that the car came down Woodrop Street, Dalmarnock, crossed a piece of waste ground and skidded into a gully before toppling over the embankment. The police believe either that the car was stolen and abandoned by thieves or that the driver was unfamiliar with the district and did not realise he had left the road. Early this morning a list of stolen cars was being examined in police headquarters and checked against the description of the car which was empty and no one was found in the river.

New Year's Day

The New Year was brought in, as it had been for the last 50 years or so, out on the river at midnight. Our December 31st was always spent, as it is in so many Glasgow households, with Mother and the girls working like slaves up to the last minute, cleaning every speck of dirt from the house, setting the table with the shortbread, the ginger wine, blackcurrant wine, cherry bun, plain bun for Father, the china and the silver teapot, the lace tablecloth and the cloth serviettes, for the midnight feast.

The next day's meals prepared, fires set all over the house, we changed our clothes and put the used ones into the washing. Father made sure that no one in the house owed anyone money – no debt is allowed to be carried into the New year – so we parted company with the odd penny that we had borrowed, probably to buy sweeties.

Half past eleven, and out the men go, into the Glasgow night air, be it hail, rain or dry, and down to the life-boats, out onto the river, to sit, floating in the still air, listening to the Scottish tunes being played on the bells of the Tron steeple: 'Maxwellton Braes', 'The Rowan Tree', 'Auld Lang Syne'.

Our pockets rattled with the goodies with which we would first foot: a bottle and shortbread for the house, to bring luck, a present for each person in the house, and a lump of black coal for the fire, to signify that the house lum would always reek.

Then there was the silence: a few minutes for complete peace, boat drifting, and mind drifting back over the year's happenings. Then the bells start chiming and every ship in the harbour sounds its siren. (When the wind is blowing in its prevailing west, the noise has been terrific, but due to the gradual moving down river of shipping, the sirens have lessened in volume over the years.)

We shake hands, and wish each other all the best for the coming year. The boat is berthed, and we walk up the brae to our house, where the door-light beckons, and ring the bell. The ladies of the house open the door, and we all shake hands and give our best wishes for prosperity, health and happiness; the coal is added to the lustre of the fire, and the presents handed out. We toast the New Year (in soft drinks), sing songs, eat shortbread, and then sit down for a family tea at the splendid table.

Sometimes this ritual would change slightly, with the arrival of some of Father's friends, or when we went across the bridge to the gatehouse to first-foot our nearest neighbours – the night gatehousemen and bakers – or when someone decided that they would rather spend the New Year in company (in hospital) than on their own, and to this effect, jumped into the river on Hogmanay, (close, of course, to Father, so they could be saved).

One evening in 1950, while tying up some boats about 11 pm, Father heard

113

a shout from the bridge and rushed up in time to stop a youth from jumping. He took him to the house and sat and talked some sense into him. He was able to go home with some of his friends.

In the same year, Father recovered the body of a woman from the River Clyde. This woman had gone missing about seven months previously in very sad circumstances. She had, it seems, taken a small amount of left-over food from her place of employment to give to her cat; this was discovered and she was given the sack. She came from a very God-fearing and proud family, and could not face the fact that her little bit of indiscretion could be thought of as theft, so she drowned herself. How things have changed money-wise in the world today; many people don't have any real sense of loyalty (or guilt if they 'acquire' something).

Early in 1951, Father had come up from the boats to get his tea. It was about 9.30 in the evening and he had been down at the boatshed all day, scraping and painting, getting his boats ready for the summer, the only interruption being when two members from one of the rowing clubs, who had gone out in a canoe, capsized and ended up in the river, shouting for help. Needless to say, they were picked up from the river, in the usual rapid fashion the river-users had come to expect from Father.

Mother had just put his meal on the table when the door bell rang and Father was told, 'Bennie, there's a woman jumped off the bridge.' Father raced down the brae, vaulted the railing and got into his boat. As he raced down river, he saw the woman lying in the water about 30 yards away. He lifted her into his boat and brought her back to consciousness. He raced back to the wharf and carried the woman to the house where Mother helped remove her wet clothes and put her to bed until the arrival of an ambulance which took her to the Royal Infirmary.

Again the work went on and on with the recoveries of the bodies of a man from the River Clyde, a ship's cook from Peterhead from the Clyde, a boy of six from the River Kelvin, and a boy of nine from the Clyde. The story of the boy from the River Kelvin, according to newspapers is as follows:

> Dusk, and the waters swirl into Glasgow's River Kelvin as a mill lade is dragged for the body of a boy. People in Kelvingrove Park, on the lower walk, opposite the waterfall, looked on helplessly as a 6 year old boy toppled off a wooden breakwater into the lade. For a moment he rose and tried to grasp the greasy plank, then he disappeared. The sluice gates of the lade which feeds the Regent Mills in Burnhouse Road were dropped. Mr. Ben Parsonage dragged the water from a boat. Further downstream near Kelvin Hall a sweep of the river was searched until a late hour without success.

Father recovered the boy's body the next day.

It was about this time in 1951 that one of the crews from the school's rowing club was caught by a gust of wind, and the five boys were thrown into the river.

Then on the sixth day of his search, Father located the body in about 40 feet of water in the centre of the river. He lifted her into his boat and covered her body with his raincoat. He rowed to the quay wall, tied his boat to the ladder and climbed up onto the dockside. Father carried in his pocket a key for the police boxes so he unlocked the box in the dockyard and phoned the police about his find, and an immediate call went out to Mr Johnstone.

Father then phoned Mother to tell her that he would be home for dinner that day. Mother still said that she could hardly believe her ears when Father phoned his message. As I said already, everyone had thought this search a lost cause. The detectives arrived and the body was lifted out and removed to the City Mortuary. The man in Barlinnie, who had originally been charged with culpable homicide, had his charge reduced to one of assault.

Later that year, in September, Father was called out to search for another woman who was suspected to have been murdered before she had been thrown in. On Thursday September 5th Father was asked to search Rothesay Dock for a woman, after her green peep-toes shoes had been found on the dockside.

A taxi had been turned back by one of four policemen who were on duty at the dock, and the occupants, a foreign-looking man and a woman with shoulder length hair, were told that no women were allowed in the dock; it was thought that the couple entered by another gate. Boatmen said that they had seen a man and woman in the dockyard and later had seen the man by himself.

After three days' search Father recovered from the river a red bucket-type shopping bag, and a handbag of imitation corded silk. Two police sergeants took possession of this, and a description was circulated in an attempt to establish the identity of the owner.

In the hope of finding a clue as to whether she was murdered or not, police interviewed many British and foreign seamen, including the crews of two ships which had left Rothesay Dock over the weekend. A third ship which left on Wednesday night was still on the high seas. A Glasgow woman came forward to say that the articles were similar to ones belonging to her daughter.

Father searched Rothesay Dock for many days but did not recover the woman. He couldn't have: she wasn't there. Her body was recovered almost two weeks later four miles further down river.

A Bad Break

In September, Father was called upon to search the River Mouse at Lanark for two men who had fallen from Gartland Bridge 180 feet into the water. His boat was lowered down by ropes, then Father and some police officers climbed down.

Parts of the ravine were very shallow, and those Father waded wearing thigh

BENJAMIN PARSONAGE (52)   Glasgow Humane Society Officer,
Humane Society House, Glasgow
Green, C.5.

states:-

    On Saturday, 24th March, 1956, I received information from
Chief Inspector Johnston, Marine Division, that a woman had been
seen to jump into the River Clyde adjacent to Meadowside Ferry
from the north bank and eastwards of the ferry.

    Same date I had my boat taken to that locus and started
dragging operations. These continued until Thursday, 29th March,
1956, during the hours of daylight.

    About 10.30 a.m. on 29th March, 1956, whilst making a
sweep about 75 yards west of Meadowside Ferry and at a position
in the river between a third and a half of the distance across
the river from the north bank, I recovered the body of a woman
and took it into my boat.

    I immediately sent word to the Marine Police Office and
Chief Inspector Johnston and Detective Inspector Duncan arrived
a short time later. The body was then removed by shell to the
city Mortuary.

Bowling Club. He phoned the police and had the raft removed. Later that evening we spotted four boys playing on a raft near King's Bridge. We phoned the police, then rushed upriver and removed the boys from the raft to the bank. Next day they had built another raft, which again we had to remove to our wharf, break up and burn.

Next day again, we came upon yet another raft with three boys playing on it at Braehead Street. Father took them off and again brought the raft to the wharf where it was broken up and burned. the boys were making these rafts from old doors and wood from houses nearby that were being demolished; they were launching them into the river at an old, overhanging tree, about three-quarters of a mile upstream of our wharf. Father arranged with the police to have the tree removed, and for any old doors etc. to be taken away.

A few weeks after the recovery of the boy from the Easterhouse conduit, Father recovered the body of yet another young boy from a similar pipe carrying the Monkland Canal below the road at Easterhouse.

141

Breaking up a raft to avert accidents

all weathers, said, 'Someone takes care of me'. He would come in after a long day of searching in snow and ice and Mother would say 'My, Bennie, what a mess your hands are in', (his hands would be cut and bleeding) and he would answer 'It's nothing, it's just the water on the ropes freezing and the ice cuts as I pass the ropes through my hands'. It never bothered him, he just accepted it as part of his job.

The same attitude applied when Mother would ask him what he had to eat all day, he would usually answer, 'I didn't bother, I wasn't hungry.' She soon learned to leave him alone regarding these matters, as he seemed quite content, and she knew she wouldn't change him. He would tackle anything. Like a lot of the older generation, I think he worked too hard.

On Hogmanay 1961 Father received a telephone call about 7 pm from the police: a watchman had been reported missing from a boat berthed at the mouth of the King George V Dock. He headed straight to the dock to survey the situation. Owing to treacherous conditions he decided to begin his search at daylight. Next day, after returning home and bringing in the New Year in the usual fashion on the river, Father resumed the search for the watchman and around noon recovered the body.

The Janet Case

January 7th, 1962 is a day which will be remembered for a long time by the legal profession in Scotland. At 5 am on that day, an incident occurred that was to lead to a trial which made legal history months later.

On January 7th 1962, at about 5 am, Father received a telephone message from a Detective Inspector of Maryhill Police. He was told that the clothes of a young girl had been found on the banks of the River Kelvin opposite Lacrosse Terrace and that it was thought that she had been murdered and thrown into the river.

I shall always remember the scene on the river bank at Lacrosse Terrace. A police car ran Father and I to the spot. As we turned into the terrace I saw the dark Glasgow night split by the staccato flashes from dozens of blue lights from the police cars, fire engines, and ambulances. The road was cordoned off; the fire brigade were setting up floodlights; the police forensic and photographic experts were bustling all over the banking. I stood beside the police car and watched as Father went forward to the spot where the clothes had been found, shaking hands with the various detectives and uniformed chiefs as they came over to speak to him.

Father viewed the River Kelvin, which was a raging torrent after the recent thaw and heavy rain. The whole day was spent searching as best he could along the immediate banking, and gradually working down river until darkness again fell.

The next day, January 8th, was spent in a similar way searching the river right down to the Clyde.

On January 9th, at about 2 pm, after a morning spent searching the Kelvin, the search dramatically switched to the Forth and Clyde Canal. Father received word from an inspector at Maryhill that the crew of a barge on the canal had seen what they thought was the body of a girl churned up in their wake. When they tried to get hold of it it disappeared beneath the surface again at a point about 150 yards east of Ruchill Bridge.

Father immediately switched the dragging operations to the Canal at this point. The search continued till 10 pm without success. On January 10th Father resumed his search of the canal at about 8 am. Arrangements were made for the barge to come back and go over the stretch were the body had been seen. The barge arrived shortly after 2 pm and, on the fourth run over the stretch, the body of a woman surfaced. Father took her into his boat and rowed to the old basin in the canal, facing Oakbank Hospital. He formed the opinion that the woman had been in the water for about three weeks and was about 40 years of age. Police identified her a few days later. The *Evening Times* of January 8th 1962 this time told the story:

'SLIPPERS' MAN ACCUSED OF MURDER. HE APPEARS IN COURT AS POLICE SEARCH KELVIN FOR JANET SMITH'S BODY.

A man wearing carpet slippers appeared at the Central Police Court Glasgow today, charged with the murder of a 4 year old Maryhill girl whose body is still missing. This afternoon the search for Janet's body switched from the river Kelvin to the River Clyde. It is believed to be the first time in Scottish legal history that a man has faced a murder charge without the body being found. Police went to the banks of the Kelvin at Lacrosse Terrace a quarter of a mile from her home. Mr Ben Parsonage patrolled the Clyde at Govan Ferry this afternoon. So did a Police Launch. Earlier Mr. Parsonage toured the River Kelvin. He said 'I think that it is very unlikely that the girl's body has floated well down river, but I don't think there is much chance of finding it today.'

On January 11th Father arrived at the River Kelvin at Maryhill. As the river was in heavy spate he found it impossible to search there, so he resumed the search at Inglis's Shipyard, near the mouth of the river several miles down, where the run was not so heavy.

On January 12th, the operations were limited to searching the side of the river due to the heavy flooding. On January 13th, at 5.45 am, Father received a call to proceed to the entrance of Kingston Dock at Shearer Street, where it was suspected that a vehicle had smashed through the gates and entered the water. He made an immediate search of the Clyde at that point and, after two hours, formed the opinion that the vehicle had never reached the water. A Clyde Trust diver was sent for, just in case. He located nothing and verified what Father had said.

Father returned to continue his search of the River Kelvin at 9.30 am. From January 14th till January 20th, from dawn till dusk, Father searched the River Kelvin. At 11.50 pm on the 20th a police car called at the house and informed Father of an accident where a woman had thrown herself into the River Clyde from the Albert Bridge. He proceeded there immediately down river by boat, and searched the area right through the night till 8.30 am without success. After a short rest, Father continued searching until dusk.

Next day he again searched for the woman at the Albert Bridge, but this woman's body wasn't to be found till several weeks later, miles down stream where she had been washed by the heavy floodwater.

On January 23rd, after a talk with Chief Superintendent White, Father made arrangements for a Clyde Trust diver to search in the River Kelvin at Henderson's Shipyard. The search was carried out in the afternoon, without success. Arrangements were made for the lade at the Co-operative Flour Mills to be drained the next day, but nothing was found there. On January 25th the Rivers Clyde and Kelvin were in heavy spate making searching difficult.

On January 26th, while Father was returning home from Maryhill in a police car, a message was radioed from the Information Room that it was rumoured that a boy might have been drowned at the ferry steps at the foot of Stag Street, Govan. Father asked the car driver to head for Govan and, after searching all evening, decided that there was no one there. the search was called off, unless the police received a report of a missing boy.

The search of the Kelvin continued. The following morning at 9.40 am Father was called on to recover the decomposed body of a man aged about 60 years from the Forth and Clyde Canal at Kelvindale Lock 21, Maryhill.

On January 31st, while Father was searching along the banks of the Kelvin in very heavy spate, he was asked by Maryhill CID to make a search of the Forth and Clyde Canal near Firhill Park for a pair of denims wanted in connection with a recent murder in Maryhill. Father recovered the denims at 3.45 pm. the search in the River Kelvin was continued next day.

On February 2nd, at 1.10 am Father received a phone message from Govan Police that a naked body had been seen floating downstream near the south of Govan Ferry. When Father arrived the police had lost sight of the body. He searched down river and, at a point opposite Balmoral Street in midstream, recovered the decomposed body of another man of about 60 years of age. The body was landed at Linthouse.

Father returned home for breakfast and, again without any sleep, at 8 am he

F

returned to the mouth of the Kelvin and continued his search for Janet. From February 3rd to 13th, he continued his search for the little girl. While searching on the 14th he received word that two bodies had been reported floating in the River Clyde. About 9 pm one body was recovered in Princes Dock, and then the other was found opposite Berth 58, Stobcross Quay, in midstream, at about 11 pm.

Father had just returned home about midnight when he received a call telling him that a body had been seen floating in the Clyde between Renfrew Ferry and Dalmuir. After a prolonged search down river, he discovered that the only bodies in the river were those of a sheep and a dog. Father was satisfied that one of those was the body reported. Headlines in the papers proclaimed: '2 found drowned in Clyde Docks riddle. Bosun who vanished from ship may be victim say Police.' Then he had to hunt for another two men.

Two men were found drowned in the River Clyde at Govan early today and police are investigating reports of two more bodies seen floating in the river at Rothesay Dock Clydebank and Renfrew Ferry. Mr. Ben Parsonage was called out in his boat to search

From February 15th till March 4th, Father searched every day in the Kelvin for Janet. At about 4.45 pm on the 4th, Father received word from the Information Room that a boy had fallen through the ice on the Forth and Clyde Canal behind Westerton Railway Station at Dumbarton.

Father and I went there immediately, with our boat on the police trailer. After breaking the ice with an axe to allow the boat through, we reached the hole through which the boy had fallen and recovered his body immediately. Father then picked up the boy's bicycle. This lad, a restaurant page boy, had been walking home pushing his red bicycle; he had strapped lengths of trimmed wood to the handlebars. Instead of using the tunnel 100 yards away, he had tried to take a short cut across the frozen canal. He tested the ice with his bike and thought it was strong enough, but half way across the ice cracked, he fell through and was drowned.

On March 5th, at about 8.30 am, Father received word that there was the body of a woman floating at Berth 16, Broomielaw. Father went there immediately and secured the body. He landed at the Clyde Trust Steps. The body, which was that of a young woman who appeared to have been in the water about seven weeks, was removed to the mortuary and Father continued down river to the Kelvin to search for the little girl.

From March 6th to 21st the search for Janet continued. On the 22nd, while he was making his way down river to the Kelvin, Father passed the dredger *Elderslie* working at Berth 52, opposite Stobcross Quay. He was very surprised to see one of the grabs pick up a motor car.

Boy's bicycle is recovered from Forth and Clyde Canal

Father rushed to the assistance of the dredger's crew, and then, with police to help, he removed the body of a man from the car.

Again his work was the subject of several newspaper stories, one which from the *Evening Times* read:

MAN IN CAR TAKEN FROM CLYDE.
The mud-covered car rests on its roof on the quayside after it was brought up from the River Clyde today. The 7 week old mystery surrounding the disappearance of a Glasgow stevedore ended today when his car was brought out of the River Clyde. His body was found jammed in the window of the car when it was fished out of the water at Stobcross Quay by the crew of a dredger. It was removed from the car by Mr. Ben Parsonage. The dead man's brother watched as the dredger's crane raised the car, a Ford Saloon, onto the dockside. The car had vanished in the fog and a search of this stretch of the river by police failed to trace it. The spot where the car was found was only about 800 yards from the shed where the drowned man worked.

On March 23rd Father continued his search for Janet. At about 6.15 pm he received word that a body had been seen floating in the River Clyde near to Rutherglen Bridge. He went there immediately and recovered the body. When he returned home, he received a call from Chief Superintendent Madill of the Marine Branch asking if he could go out the next morning to search for a missing Drumchapel boy. One newspaper reported:

Police may circulate hundreds of pictures of a 13 year old boy who vanished 5 days ago. Police and Mr. Ben Parsonage searched the Forth And Clyde Canal near the boy's home. Police with tracker dogs combed the woods and fields. Police all over the country have been asked to look out for the boy, and a police spokesman in Glasgow said today 'We are doing all we can to find the boy. We have no clue to where he is. If only we knew where to look we might have a chance.'

From March 24th to April 1st Father searched the canal and the locks at Drumchapel. On April 2nd, the murder trial of Francis John Edward Kilbride took place at the High Court, and the *Glasgow Herald* of April 4th 1962 took up the story:

KILBRIDE IMPRISONED FOR LIFE.
Before Lord Strachan and a jury at Glasgow, Francis John Edward Kilbride was sent to prison for life when a jury, by a majority found him guilty of the murder on January 6 of 4 year old Janet Smith whose body had never been recovered from the River Kelvin in Glasgow. One of the last witnesses for the crown, Mr. Ben Parsonage, Officer of the Glasgow Humane Society said that of hundreds of

● *AS POLICE wait on the bank, Mr Ben Parsonage recovers the child's body from the River Kelvin.*

searches he had made during his 32 years service he had known of only one
other case in which a body had not been recovered from the River Kelvin.
The River Kelvin was a raging torrent on January 6th with heavy rain after a fast
thaw.

The search continued, the only other interruption being to recover the body of a
man from the Clyde at Mavisbank Quay, until May 15th, when the body of Janet
Smith was finally found in the River Kelvin, a few yards north of the footbridge at
the bandstand in Kelvinbridge Park.

And so the months-long saga was concluded in the newspapers:

MURDERED CITY CHILD FOUND IN RIVER KELVIN SIX WEEKS AFTER HER KILLER IS JAILED FOR
LIFE.
Ben Parsonage took a dinghy on to the river and brought the body to the shore.
It was wrapped in a coat on the grass bank. Later, an ambulance arrived to take
it to the mortuary, from the night she went missing until this afternoon Glasgow
Police and Mr. Ben Parsonage have searched for the body of Janet Smith.

Kilbrides's sentence turned out to be for life, for in August 1978, he died of a heart
attack two hours after arriving back in Saughton Prison from Edinburgh Royal
Infirmary, where he had been for ten days after an earlier heart attack.

After these four months of constant work, the normal business that went on
must have seemed very easy to Father, but go on it did, bodies being recovered,
hoaxes being investigated, accidents being prevented and all the usual incidents
ocurring.

CHAPTER 13

The Early Sixties

In September 1962 a little girl was drowned at the mouth of the River Kelvin, and a search, similar in some ways to, but by no means as spectacular as, the Janet case, took place. From September 17th till October 5th a daily search was made of the River Clyde,with a few interruptions for the recovery of bodies elsewhere.

On October 5th the girl's body was recovered by Father during grappling operations in the River Clyde at Merklands Quay, which is just a short distance down river from Meadowside. This was quite a remarkable piece of recovery work by Father, as no one could tell the spot where the girl had fallen in. Also, the currents and the depth of water in the area would, I think, have made a proper search impossible. But 19 days of patient and methodical dragging up and down the same stretch of river were finally rewarded when Father recovered the girl's body. The *Evening Times* of September 17th told the story:

CLYDE RIDDLE OF SCREAMING TEENAGER.
A 13 year old girl stumbled screaming from the icy Clyde last night and started a full scale hunt that went on until after midnight, for she told the police that a man had attacked her and her young cousin and had thrown them into Meadowside Quay at Partick, Glasgow. Police with tracker dogs and torches searched the quayside. Mr. Ben Parsonage was also called out to drag the dark river. The drama began when two boys heard screams from the side of the water. They ran to investigate and found a 13 year old girl lying sobbing on a grass bank. She said she had been attacked. The boys carried her to a post office nearby where she said her friend was 'floating down the river'. A Senior official at Glasgow Marine Police Station said later 'Foul play has not yet been ruled out. It may be an accident, but the facts of the case are not clear and the CID are confirming their investigations.'

Later it was decided that this girl's drowning had been accidental.

In January 1963 the police telephoned Father to ask for his assistance at West Street where it was thought that a vehicle had been driven into the river. In a very short time Father had launched his boat at the Finnieston Ferry steps and rowed upriver to Windmillcroft Quay. The police on the quay wall told him the story of

• Mr Ben Parsonage drags the Clyde to-day, near Meadowside
Ferry, Partick, Glasgow.

what had happened. The car had crashed through a steel chain barrier, raced across 20 yards of frosty cobbled quay and plunged 20 feet into the Clyde. Although the car had stayed afloat for fully five minutes, the driver had made no attempt to get out.

Father climbed up a ladder onto the quay wall and viewed the scene, examining the tell-tale tyre marks, and decided at which spot he thought the car would lie. After about half an hour he located the vehicle. He anchored his boat to the car until the arrival of a Clyde Trust diver who went down the ropes and fastened wire hawsers round the vehicle, enabling the mobile crane that had arrived to lift it from the water.

Once the car was on the quay wall, Father removed the body of a man from the driver's seat. The body was removed to the City Mortuary where a post mortem revealed that the man had died of a heart attack, probably before the car had crashed through the barrier.

Then, on January 18th, police phoned to say that a vehicle was on its way to take Father to the Monkland Canal at Castle Street where an 8-year-old boy had been drowned when he crashed through the ice into the freezing water. The gates were opened and the boat wheeled out, just in time to meet the police van, and they sped off into the dark Glasgow night, lights flashing and sirens blaring.

The scene at the canal was a riot of activity, motor car headlights danced on the ice, showing where it was broken by pickaxes and the hands of those who had tried to get the boy. A hole still showed in the ice where the youngster had sunk. The boat was slid off the trailer and willing hands launched it across the ice to the hole. After a few minutes Father brought the boy's body to the surface. A waiting ambulance took the boy the short distance to the Royal Infirmary but he was beyond all help. Again local residents demanded that the canal be filled in and, sure enough, today the Castle Street M8 junction is on this spot, traffic flowing where water once did.

The next day Father was called to the Clyde at the George V Dock, where Govan Police were trying to trace a watchman who had been missing for a few days.

Father searched the Clyde in the area where the watchman made his rounds. While he was searching he received word that there was a body in the river at Glasgow Green. He returned to the Green and recovered the decomposed body of a man from the river at Waddell Street. For eight days Father searched the King George V Dock without success. The man's body was recovered a few weeks later in another part of the river.

On February 21st, Father received word that a boy had fallen into the River Cart 200 yards from the Pollok Estate. He proceeded there immediately and recovered the body of a 16-year-old boy. The boy was 15 seconds from safety, according to one newspaper report:

Ben anchors his boat to a car

15 seconds ticked away – that was the desperate margin between life and death for a boy in an ice-covered river last night. 15 seconds as he jumped up and down on the river bed in a desperate attempt to keep his head above water. 15 seconds as a man on the bank hacked at a sapling in a bed to pull him to safety. 15 seconds too late.

Father recovered the body after 20 minutes search. As he searched, lying on the ice near the bank was tragic evidence of the boy's swift plunge to death – his spectacles, resting on the two-inch thick ice.

One March night, as we were settling down for the night, we heard the noise of a car braking outside and rushed downstairs in time to open the door to a policeman: 'Bennie, there's a man has only a few minutes ago jumped off Rutherglen Bridge.'

Knowing how fast the river was flowing with the heavy floodwater that was coming down, Father ran for the lifeboat. With me hard on his heels he ran down the brae and over the fence. As I jumped into the bow seat, Father slipped the painter and we raced out into the raging currents; heading across stream and picking up the eddy on the south bank we moved upriver.

As we approached the King's Bridge Father's hawk-like eyes spotted something suspicious floating down river, just breaking the surface. Indeed it was the man's body. He brought it over the gunwhales into the boat and started applying artificial respiration. A shout to the police on the bank and a quick radio message changed the direction of the ambulance, en route for Rutherglen Bridge, to our wharf in the Green, and with the 'Minute Man' in action (a portable resuscitator), the man was taken with a police escort to the Royal Infirmary where, unfortunately, he was found to be dead. It was a sad ending, but another example of Father's unique knowledge as he almost pulled off the impossible. Rutherglen Bridge is one mile from our wharf.

April came, and Father, after a short search, recovered the body of a watchman who had fallen overboard from the dredger *Craigie Hall* berthed at Queens Dock. A few days later he had to rush upstream in his speedboat when it was reported that the body of a woman was floating near to the Dalmarnock Power Station. Father recovered the body from the grids in front of the power station intake. She had only been a few hours in the water.

In May Father recovered a car from the Clyde near Yoker Power Station for the police. Vehicles were taken from the river or just located for the police so often that records were never kept. It's amazing to think that Father actually lifted a Triumph 500 motor bike and sidecar into his boat!

Later in the month an ice cream van went into the River near Millerfield Road. Father and I went there immediately. The police passed a wire rope from a Corporation breakdown waggon, which Father fastened to the rear of the van. The breakdown waggon pulled the van out of the water up the high bank on to the road. Luckily there was no one inside the van which proved to have been stolen.

Blackie

Then on May 25th, 1963, Father noted in his diary 'Rescued dog stranded on the pier of the Albert Bridge. Decided to keep dog, named it Albert.' And the *Scottish Daily Express* proclaimed:

ONE BARK TO HAPPINESS!
Blackie, the stray snatched from river peril. Blackie the two month old collie pup will never forget the night, the night he was snatched to safety from the middle of the swirling River Clyde to find happiness in a new home. For hours Blackie crouched wet and shivering on the base of a concrete pillar beneath the Albert Bridge, Saltmarket, Glasgow, bravely barking to attract attention. At first, as the dark flowing river rushed past him Blackie's position looked hopeless. then a passer-by heard his plaintive yelps and called the police. Within minutes the police accompanied by Mr. Ben Parsonage and his son George arrived off the quayside from Glasgow Green with a small rowing boat. Although weakened by the cold, exposure and lack of food, Blackie still managed to wag his tail as the small boat with his rescuers approached. Mr. Parsonage only had to stretch out his hand and without waiting to be asked a second time Blackie jumped into his arms. Then it was straight back to the Glasgow Green where a happy whimpering Blackie was given a rub-down and some milk. Mr. Ben Parsonage had taken a fancy to the dog and offered to look after 'Albert' for the statutory 30 days and to keep him if no one claimed him.

•• SAVED: Blackie rescued from river ledge.

During November 1963 there was a terribly heavy rain. Father worked hard putting extra ropes on the barges and lifeboats, lifting all extra boats out of the water, tying down all movable objects around the sheds, and even the sheds, in case the water rose and they floated away.

During a flood years ago, Father's friends tell of the day the water rose high enough to float the boatshed. Father entered the swirling water, and swam with a rope around the shed, pulled it onto high ground and tied it up safely to the surrounding trees. When the water went down, he set to with a terrific 'well it happened' attitude, laid a new base for the shed, gradually levered it back into position, and repaired it.

He took all this in his stride. Mother told the story of the tide being so high one day that Father's sandwiches were washed from the bench were they were lying, four feet up in the boatshed!

This November, Father may have been ready for the ensuing flood, but other river users weren't, and at 3 am Father received word that motor launches were floating loose on the river. These proved to be the boats from the Rutherglen Motor Boat club, loosed from their moorings by the heavy spate of the river. Father did everything he could to stop their passage but failed, so strong was the current. Many boats ended up smashed on the bridges and at the weir gates. Because of the currents it was difficult for Father to carry out the searches he had to make in the River Clyde during the next few days. On November 17th he received word at about 8 am that a boy was missing from his home in Maryhill and was possibly in the water. Father proceeded there immediately, and searched till dusk. He was out all day and must have been tired when he reached his bed that night, but he wasn't to get much sleep for at about 11.35 pm he was told by the Maryhill police that a person had been drowned in the Forth and Clyde Canal at the Firhill basin. He went there immediately, and after a few minutes' search he recovered a man's body.

Father then returned to his search for the boy at Maryhill, which was concentrated on the River Kelvin. He found marks on the river bank which could have been made by someone falling. Chief Detective Inspector Robert Macfarlane, head of Maryhill CID, accompanied by Detective Inspector John MacDonald, also of Maryhill, were called to the scene, went out with Father in his boat, and spent some time examining the spot, which was directly opposite a hole in the fence through which the boy had been playing. The detectives said the marks indicated that the boy might have fallen in at the river at this point. His body was recovered in the River Clyde near Blythswood Shipyard.

The Glasgow ferry dolphins were made of wooden piling which, in later years, became in need of repair, with planks broken and missing.

One February day, Father was called to the River Clyde at the end of Lancefield Quay, where a body had been spotted floating behind the piles. At about 11 am, Father lay over the quay wall, and dropping ropes down through the broken piling, managed to tie them around the body of a woman. He then discovered that there was no way of removing the body from its position with the prevailing state of the tide.

Father told the police that, when the tide rose to its highest, he might manage to bring the body out without marking it. This was agreed and a long wait ensued. In fact it was about 11 pm that night before the tide returned to a high enough level for Father to complete the recovery.

The usual work continued, with bodies being recovered at the weir, Firhill Basin, Hogganfield Loch, the canal at Garscadden, George V Bridge, Finnieston Ferry, Malls Mire, Jamaica Bridge, Knightswood Bridge, Glasgow, Temple Bridge, and eight or nine people who fell into the river were brought out safely in Father's 'make-it-look-simple' fashion.

As the summer approached, Father gave this warning to holidaymakers via the *Sunday Post*:

> Last night Ben Parsonage gave this warning to the thousands of Scots holidaymakers who'll soon be flocking to the beaches 'Never stand up in a craft. If you have to change seats then make for the nearest landing stage, the few minutes this takes could save lives. If you fall overboard, or your boat capsizes stay with the boat till rescue comes. Ninety-nine out of 100 boats won't sink. Hold on to the boat and don't panic. When you see youngsters on a raft in deep water, phone the police or coastguards.'

It was at this time that I discovered just how well Father had drummed into me how to react to a situation, when I had the privilege to rescue an elderly woman who had fallen from St Andrew's Suspension Bridge into the river. She was taken to the house, where the Parsonage team again swung into full action, and the woman was sitting up in bed waiting for the ambulance. The rescue made Father very proud.

The pattern seldom changed, as the following newspaper stories show:

'Is there any hope? Heartbreak father asks – then missing son is found dead in killer canal.'

'He had been well warned.'

'Boy, 10 vanished on an errand.'

'A little boy missing from his home for nearly three days was found drowned this afternoon in the killer Forth And Clyde Canal. The 10-year-old boy was pulled from the water by Mr. Ben Parsonage who was near to tears as his boat was rowed to the canal bank.'

'Two boys see man plunge into river. Two 8 year old boys were playing near the River Kelvin on Friday, when they saw a man fall into the water. They gave the alarm. Mr. Ben Parsonage was called out and the river was dragged. A body was recovered from the river and later identified.'

'Toddler in pit horror'

During December 1965 Father was called to Queens Dock on the River Clyde where the cook was reported to have fallen off the motor vessel *Firth Fisher* at 10.30 pm. Father raced to the locus and recovered the body between the ship and the quay wall.

The day after Father had been called to take the body of a man from the Forth and Clyde Canal at Kelvin Docks, Maryhill, he was called again to almost the same locus. One paper reported:

A father collapsed in tears as he watched dragging operations in a Canal last night. For hours he had stood on the Canal bank hoping that the boy they searched for was not his son. But his hopes were in vain. The long vigil ended last night when the five year old's body was recovered by Ben Parsonage, police and ambulance armed with grappling hooks tried for about an hour in a vain attempt to locate the boys' body before Mr. Parsonage was called in.

On Friday October 1st, 1965 Father was called to Plantation Quay. Hundreds of Belfast-bound soccer fans on the 'Royal Scotsman', due to sail for Ireland, had seen a young man plunge into the water from a ship – the *Megantic* – moored nearby. Within seconds he had disappeared below the surface.

A check on crew members of the *Megantic* had been carried out, and a fire boat searched for the man. The Irish boat, also on the lookout, had been delayed for 20 minutes. Father continued his search all through Saturday and Sunday.

The police said that at the time they had no clue to the youth's identity, and added: 'No crew members of the *Megantic* are missing.' They found some clothing aboard but didn't know to whom it belonged. The body was recovered by Father after a long search, which was frequently interrupted with cases like the following:

A middle-aged man was found on a ledge by the riverside at Govan. The man had been in the river for some time, and was probably left lying on the ledge as the tide went out. When Father was called to recover this body he found it lying spreadeagled over the piles on the river bank. The body was badly decomposed and it took a lot of skill and hard work to lift it clear without it falling to bits.

Christmas Day 1965, Father was out searching for, and recovering, the body of a man from the River Kelvin at the rear of the art galleries.

Hogmanay, 10.20 pm, when the family was putting the finishing touches to the New Year preparations, the door bell rang, and when he opened it a man

173

collapsed into Father's arms. He was carried into the treatment room where Father removed his wet clothing, tended to him and made him as comfortable as possible until the arrival of the ambulance which took him to hospital. At 11.58 pm the ambulance left, and they brought the New Year in in the ambulance!

We brought the New Year in with mop-pails and brushes and happiness. The man had been released from Erskine Hospital that day and, realising that he had no real place to go at New Year, thought he would jump in the river. He waded in, but the cold water changed his mind, and he came out to Father for help.

January 2nd brought another sad incident. Father was called to the Monkland Canal at Gala Street to recover the body of a new-born male child which was floating in the water.

On March 23rd, Father dragged the River Kelvin under the bridge at Maryhill below the gap in the parapet covered by fencing, where a car had crashed. Father found the body of a young man after about a 12-hour search. Police had found the car hanging over the bridge in Skaethorn Road, Maryhill. After it was discovered that the driver was not at home it was decided to search the river. The man was identified as a former Scotland and Celtic football star.

On Monday March 29th 1966 at 9.30 am Father received a call from the County police that a boy of 2 years was reported missing, and was thought to have fallen into the River Cart. After a two-day search, Father recovered the body from the river 100 yards south of the bridge in Linn Park in a 12-foot deep pool.

Tommy

The end of May 1966 brought another search that was to last many weeks and cover a lot of ground. On May 27th Father received word from Govan police that a boy was missing in their area and it was suspected that he had fallen into the River Clyde. On May 28th he searched all day for the boy at Govan. On May 29th he rescued a man from the Clyde then continued the search at Govan. On May 30th he searched at Govan again. At 1.30 pm Father received word that the body of a man had been seen floating in the river near to the George V Bridge. Father rowed upstream and recovered the body. He returned to Govan and continued his search for the boy.

On June 1st while still searching at Govan, Father received a call, at about 5.45 pm, that a man had been drowned at the foot of Hydepark Street. He searched mostly under the quay behind the piles, until midnight when he had to stop searching because the tide was rising so fast that it was trapping his boat beneath the quay.

During the days of the search for the Govan boy, the *Glasgow Herald* and *Evening Times* carried the following report:

In addition to the river search police are again concentrating in the immediate vicinity of the boy's home. All this has been done before but police officers feel he may still be in the area. Neighbouring police divisions have also been alerted to look out for Tommy. A house-to-house search of the area and of the Clyde Tunnel has yielded no trace of the youngster. Police have already received reports from the public of sightings of Tommy from places as far away as Edinburgh. In addition, ponds in Elder Park, Govan and in Victoria Park on the other side of the Clyde were searched with no result. A pool of water in a timber yard near Shieldhall Dock was pumped out by firemen.

On June 2nd 1966 Father returned to Hydepark Street at 4.30 am, when the tide had dropped sufficiently to allow his boat back under the wharf, and after a short search recovered the body of a Clyde Trust worker in about 10 feet of water. He went downstream and continued the search for the boy at Govan.

On June 3rd the search continued. At about 10.45 pm our phone rang and the police informed me that a man had drowned when he had jumped off the Clyde Street Ferry, and tried to swim to the bank. As Father was still at Govan, I went with the police to Clyde Street, while notification of the accident was sent to Father. After a few minutes search I recovered the body. Father arrived as I brought the body to the surface and took over the removal of the body from the water.

On June 4th and 5th he searched all day at Govan, then on June 6th, he recovered the boy's body. At about 8.45 pm he returned home. Father then received a call that a man was suspected to have fallen into the river this time at Govan Ferry. After a short search he recovered the body.

Just after dinner on July 2nd, at about 1.15 pm, Father received a call from Govan police that a boy of 8 had been reported missing from his home since 2.30 pm the previous day and could not be found anywhere in the vicinity. There was a chance that he might have fallen into the River Cart. Father proceeded there immediately and started searching likely places. At around 5 pm the policeman on the riverbank received a call over his radio that the body of a man had been spotted floating down the Clyde next to Berth 57, Mavisbank Quay. The boat was lifted from the River Cart onto the trailer and taken across the city and launched at Mavisbank. After a short search he recovered the body of an American from Brooklyn, New York, at 5.30 pm. The police conveyed Father and the boat back to the Cart where at about 9 pm, he recovered the body of the boy from the water.

175

CHAPTER 14

The Tidal Weir

A few weeks later, it had been a lovely summer's day and Father and I were packing up the boats for the night, putting oars and rowlocks away, shutters on the shed windows, checking the lifeboats, all our usual routine, when the phone rang: it was the Police Information Room to say that a man had jumped off the Albert Bridge into the water. Father and I leapt into the lifeboat and double-sculled as only we two could downstream.

What happened next I shall never forget as long as I live. The water on the downside of the weir gate was too low to allow the gates to be lifted and to allow us to use our ramp. Father seemed to be able to assess all this without even looking around, he just knew: a sixth sense. We always approached anything stern first, and we spun the boat around, stern-on-to the gate. I followed Father's instructions without thinking, although, looking back, I shall never forget this: he stepped briskly out of the boat on to the one-inch wide weir gate, balancing himself against the boat, and shouted at me to do the same on the other side. We eased the stern over the gate, and let the boat see-saw, slide and drop the 9 feet down into the swirling water behind the weir. As it dropped, Father shouted for me to jump into the boat, then he stood balanced in mid air for a few seconds, before he leapt and joined me in the boat.

We rowed out of the swirling water, and in mid-stream, found three men hanging onto a lifebelt, two on the outside supporting one on the inside. The two men had seen a man floundering in the water and dived in to try to save him. All three were lifted into our boat, and artificial respiration was applied to the man who had been in the middle of the lifebelt. We reached the bank, and the ambulance took over the resuscitation without avail: the man had been under the water for too long. All three were taken to the Royal Infirmary. Our boat was carried round the weir, and we rowed home. Why will I never forget that? – just have a look some time at the weir gate!

Again it is worth looking at a newspaper report of the day, July 16th, 1966:

Two rescuers almost lost their lives last night trying to save a man who had plunged 40 feet from a city bridge. Later police were full of praise for the two

The river at the weir can be a raging torrent

rescuers and a boatman who shot a weir in a three-minute, half-mile race to save the drowning man. A crowd of several hundred watched the drama in the River Clyde beneath Albert Bridge in the heart of Glasgow. One of the rescuers, Desmond a joiner, said later 'It was the longest few minutes in my life,' and Liam, a bookmaker's clerk, added 'I couldn't have held on much longer.'

August 11th 1966 was a typical day for Father. He was up early and, as usual, first thing in the morning went down to the boats for a look round to make sure everything was all right. He discovered one of his lifeboats had been taken away during the night. Taking oars and another boat he rowed upstream and at 6.30 am he found the boat lying on the bank at Rutherglen. After his breakfast Father went to Govan to continue a search of the river. While home for his dinner, he was told that a boy had fallen on the spikes while climbing a fence at the swings in the park. I went with Father and helped the boy to our house where he was tended to until the arrival of the ambulance to take him to hospital where his wound was stitched. Father returned to Govan where, about 5.30 pm, while still searching, he received word that a boy had been drowned when he fell into the pond at the Kelvindale Paper Mills. He was rushed from Govan to Kelvinside where I met him. After a short search, at about 6.20 pm Father recovered the body of the 9-year-old boy.

A few days later the Clyde had one of the heavy floods which makes it one of the most dangerous rivers in Europe. Father became a real expert at judging rainfall. He had lost so many boats in the past and we had managed to lift all our boats from the water and even the lifeboats were on the barge. At midnight the wall of water came round the bend. Father, as usual, stayed up all night watching the river and his beloved boats.

On October 19th Father received word that a policeman who had entered the River Clyde at the Glasgow Bridge to try rescue a woman was himself in need of help. Father let me go down to the locus on my bicycle to give any help that I could while he phoned the tidal weir attendant to lift his gates as the tide was almost level, then rushed down river in his motor boat and arrived at the scene in time to help me to the quay wall with the policeman. I had found a ship's lifeboat and paddled it out to the policeman.

After the policeman had been taken away by ambulance Father searched down river and recovered the body of the woman still floating a few inches below the surface at Berth 29, Springfield Quay about 9.50 pm. The woman was taken by ambulance to the infirmary where she was certified dead. One newspaper read:

A policeman clung to a tiny platform in the middle of a river last night after a vain bid to rescue a drowning woman. .... soaking wet the policeman clung waiting to be rescued. His cries for assistance brought patrol cars racing from other parts of the city. Ben Parsonage and his son George were called to the scene. George Parsonage commandeered a rowing boat, but there were no oars, a plank was found in the quayside and was used to canoe the boat into the river against the strong current. The constable, shivering with cold, was helped down into the swaying rowing boat. Inch by inch the boat was edged to the side helped by Mr. Parsonage who had come downstream in his boat.

Again the work went on, with cases in the Rouken Burn, and in the Clyde harbour, a boy from the grids of Dalmarnock Power Station, Tollcross Burn, and Braehead Power Station. He also went as far as Lochwinnoch, where he recovered the body of a 15-year-old boy from the River Calder.

Then one night the phone rang and, as usual, it was a scramble to answer it. The telly was flicked off, and we all stood on full alert as Father picked up the receiver. 'All stations go, woman in river at the Jamaica Bridge' – as we heard these words we also heard the slamming of car doors as a squad car which had been sitting just along from the house and had heard the message on their radio made its presence known at the front of the house. Father and I slid into the rear seats and, with wheels screaming and siren blaring, the car raced along a path and onto the carriageway. Now this was mid-December, and at the spot where the carriageway meets Greendyke Street there are cobblestones which can be like a sheet of glass with frost on them. As the speeding car's wheels touched the ice, it slid with almost a mind of its own across the road, around and around – two and a half turns without hitting anything, then a three-point turn and off again, as fast as possible, to the locus of the accident.

The car sped safely and accurately through the traffic lights and traffic jams along Clyde Street and, as it jerked to a halt at the Jamaica Bridge, we jumped out, Father leading the race toward the quay wall, still in time to help organise the lifting of the woman from the water, and aid in her resuscitation.

This was not a dramatic case for Father: the woman had really been rescued before we got there, Father only really expedited her removal to hospital, but it shows how the combination of his ability and readiness at all times, and the alertness and superb driving of the police could be fast enough to save life even at a distance.

One newspaper story in 1967 read:

WANTON DAMAGE TO LIFEBELTS.
Mr. Ben Parsonage said yesterday that vandals were responsible for the wholesale destruction of lifebelts beside the Clyde in central Glasgow. Mr. Parsonage's criticism came 24 hours after rescue attempts failed to save a man from the river at the Albert Bridge. After he was seen to fall from the bridge a passer-by tried to throw a lifebelt but could not free it from its moorings

A lifebelt vandalised may mean a life lost

because its rope was knotted. Mr. Parsonage said 'The damage to lifebelts on this stretch of the Clyde is disgraceful.' Mr. Parsonage recovered the body.

Hoodoo

Some time ago I told the story of the 'Hoodoo' ships but in my research on Father's cases for 1967, I came across the following story which I had completely forgotten.

Father received word around 10.45 pm that a watchman had fallen from the gangway of the *Tasmanian Star* and drowned. The ship was moored at Berth 16, Princess Dock. Father and I went immediately to the dock and Father started searching from the dockside between the quay and the ship. This is a very difficult way to search, but about 1 am Father recovered the body of the watchman. It really makes one wonder about the hoodoo theory.

A few days later, Father again searched between a ship and the quay wall and recovered a man's body. This time it was in Yorkhill Dock and the man was from the crew of the SS *Industria*. After bringing the man's body to the surface, Father had to descend a ladder between the ship and the quay wall in order to fasten the body up to enable it to be lifted out. This is incredibly dangerous to do because the ships move against the wall with the tide and wind, and the slightest movement in your direction could crush you to pulp.

Perhaps I shouldn't add this postscript to the 'Hoodoo' story, but early in 1979, as I was in the early stages of writing this book, Father and I were called to Govan to search for a crewman who had fallen into the dock near his ship.

The man from Liverpool had been returning to his ship after celebrating England's victory over Scotland at Wembley. After having recovered the body, we were chatting to the senior officer of the vessel and I asked him what line they were, because I had not seen the colours they had on their funnel before, and he told me it was the Starman Line, a link-up of two companies, the Man Line, and yes you've guessed it, the Star Line. What a coincidence!

New Year, 1968

I wonder how most of you feel at 7 am on a New Year's day. For many reasons, I am sure that few of us would feel like getting up at that time, but that was the hour on January 1st, 1968 that Father was called to the River Clyde at Renfrew Ferry on the Yoker side, where a motor car had run into the Clyde and trapped a woman occupant. Father proceeded there immediately, and after a short search he located the motor car. He gave a rope to one of the police sub-aqua unit, who fastened it to the woman. He then raised her to the surface, lifted her into his boat and landed her at the ferry, from where she was taken to the City Mortuary.

Next day he recovered the body of a woman from the Kelvin and on January 3rd he rescued a woman who waded into the Clyde.

Later in the month detectives raced to a city park when Father recovered the body of a young woman and an empty pram from the River Kelvin. The woman, in her late 20s, was recovered at Kelvingrove Park. A blue and white baby's pram was recovered from the water beside her.

The police did not know who the woman was, nor if there had been a baby in the pram. After a search it was decided that there was no link between the pram and the woman.

The Islands in the Clyde

There are two or three islands in the River Clyde and they can be very dangerous for anyone using them. Five boys were very lucky when they went camping on one of these islands in 1968. The River Clyde, owing to heavy rain, rose about seven feet, and the island was in danger of being covered. The boys could not swim ashore due to the severity of the flooding. A monk from the nearby monastery heard their shouts and notified the County Police, who phoned Father.

With sirens blaring, the Land Rover towing the trailer sped through the crowds dispersing after the Celtic match at Parkhead, and out the London Road to the 'County', as we called Lanarkshire. Father and I scanned the scene as we screeched to a halt on the river bank opposite the island. The Clyde was a raging torrent against which it was debatable if even Father and I could have rowed, but fortunately we had a heavy outboard with us. The ropes holding the boat onto the trailer were thrown aside, and willing hands lifted the boat to where Father wanted it launched about 50 yards above the island. He knew that the current was so fast that we would have to be pushed out bow first into the current with the engine already started and moving diagonally across the fast-moving water, the boat would come alongside the island. He had judged it perfectly, and the excited, eager waiting hands of the youths caught hold of the boat as it swept onto the now marshy edge of the isle. Father explained quickly that he would only be able to take them ashore two at a time. If the boat were loaded too deeply, it would hit any submerged rocks or old tree trunks on the bottom of the river and with the speed of the stream, that could have capsized the boat.

The youths, although frightened, accepted this with cheerfulness, for they realised that dry land was only a few minutes away. With two safely on board, the boat was shoved out again bow first into the stream and, driving diagonally again, we landed about 50 yards downstream of the island. The boat was lifted out speedily, as the water was rising all the time, and carried upstream to where it had been launched initially and the whole procedure repeated. Three trips later the grateful lads and their camping equipment were safely on the bank chatting and joking about the affair in their relief. The whole operation had been performed so speedily that our boat was back on the trailer for the return journey to the Green in less than an hour.

One Monday in April, the cry went up that a boy of five had fallen into the Clyde, just down river of Polmadie Bridge. Father rushed upriver to the scene, but the boy had disappeared. After one and a half hours' search, he recovered the body of the boy 30 yards west of Dixon's Pump and 14 feet from the South Bank.

Young boys continued to have a fatal fascination for water, and again part of Father's work at this time was the recovery of the body of an 8-year-old boy from the Forth And Clyde Canal at Knightswood.

Safety First

One of the things that Father did was to chase adults, as well as children, from lying on the banks inside the fencing. He had quite a job at times convincing them that this was for their own safety.

Father rowed down river one August day in 1968, and landed his boat on the banking below where a drunk man was lying 'sleepin' it off'. He woke him up, helped him over the fence and laid him down on the grass, in a situation where he at least wouldn't roll or stumble into the river.

This happened dozens of times over the years. Proof of its value was seen also in 1968, when a middle-aged man lying asleep rolled down the steep bank of the river into the water. By coincidence I was passing in a racing boat at the time. We took the racing boat alongside Father's lifeboats at his wharf nearby, and I jumped out and found Father, who had heard the shouts of alarm and together we rowed to the man's rescue. he was taken to our house where he was dried, put to bed, and looked after until the arrival of an ambulance to take him to hospital.

People do not always react favourably to being asked to leave the banks, like the night I saw a man and a woman, obviously the worse for drink, staggering along the banks. I asked them to leave, and, after much shouting and swearing from them, they agreed. They climbed over the fence onto the road, and I turned and walked off in the direction of the club. Fortunately, I was suddenly aware of footsteps running behind me and there was this man, with an open razor, shouting and swearing. Well, I ran as fast as I could to the Clubhouse, and only looked back when I reached the door a quarter of a mile away, by which time, having been shown a clean pair of heels, the man had gone back to join his girl. Father often mentioned incidents like this, but experiencing the incident I have just related made me appreciate even more what he had to put up with.

An 11-year-old boy was drowned in the Forth and Clyde Canal in October while he and a friend were trying to retrieve an old rubber tyre from the water. Father recovered his body after a short search. Even today we see dozens of tyres floating down the river – hardly a week passes without tyres bobbing around. I hope, having read the above story, that people will stop throwing articles like this into the water.

In November Father recovered the body of a man from the River Clyde at Anderston Quay. In the man's pocket was a brown leather wallet, which contained a blind man's pass. Sadly, it appeared that the man had taken a wrong turning and stumbled into the river without anyone noticing. It is worth mentioning at this point how angry Father got when he saw anyone leaving a gate open anywhere along the river banking, even for a short time. His words were 'You never know when a blind man will come along that road and, thinking he has reached the bridge, turn and fall into the water.' Even in this little detail, Father's life was geared towards safety.

Again Father was out on Christmas Day, this time at 6 am to search for a man who had fallen between his ship and the quay wall. The search had to be abandoned after a few hours due to the high winds crashing the ship against the quay. The man's body was recovered by Father on December 29th after a 5-day search. He recovered the body about half an hour after the ship had sailed, about 15 feet out from the quay wall, so the ship must have been floating right on top of the body.

1969 started off with Father being called to Millerfield Road, where some youths had reported seeing a leg among some debris on the river. Father went upstream in the motor boat, but found nothing: the boys must have been mistaken.

I can't understand why people cannot leave things that don't belong to them alone, especially when these things are lifebelts, fire alarms, lifeboats, etc. Father, at times, must have been really frustrated at the number of incidents of drunks taking away the lifeboats, chaps in the middle of the night taking their girlfriend for a 2 am row or 'neds' just letting the boats loose for fun, or trying to damage them – like the time he found his lifeboats at 6 am, lying across the gates of the weir, one boat across the girders with its planking damaged. Sometimes they put holes in the boats, sometimes they rowed six or seven miles upstream and ditched them, sometimes the loosened boat went over the weir gates in the dark and smashed, oars were lost, rowlocks and grapnels thrown in. If we took the oars out they would rip up the floor boards to use as paddles. The boats are chained and padlocked now, and we have emergency arrangements for their constant use but for obvious reasons they are known only to the family and the police.

The November Floods

November 1969 brought weather that has become familiar to the people of Glasgow: flooding. Father was asked to take his lifeboat to Househillwood to evacuate some people from their houses, as they were being flooded out by the rising waters of the Brock and Levern Burns. Father and I went there immediately and evacuated a mother, who was due to go into hospital, and her three children from their home. As the water seemed to have reached its highest, people decided to stay put for the time being. We stood by with the police until the water reached a safe level.

Newspaper headlines said: 'Glasgow families flee' and told of a 70 mile an hour gale ripping through Scotland. One paper tells of Father, just before midnight, sailing up Houshillwood Road with the Salvation Army officers and taking people from their homes, which were under 5 feet of water in Haughburn Road, to the local church hall, which was opened as a refugee centre.

The year ended the way it started, with Father out on the river on Hogmanay, recovering the body of a man from the Clyde at Merklands.

February 1970 brought another sad accident, when a little boy was feared to have drowned under the ice on the Forth And Clyde Canal. this little boy had rescued his friend from the canal when his friend fell in, then fell in himself, but no one could help him. Police from Glasgow and Dunbartonshire were involved in the search, and searchlights were set up to aid them. Father was called in, and searched till late that night without success. There was a 3-inch covering of ice on the canal. Next day, in terrible weather, Father continued his search and finally recovered the boy's body. The parents and their neighbours were very angry at another drowning in the canal, and were heard saying 'How long must we live with this threat?'

Youngsters kept falling into waterways: a boy into the Black Cart, and another into the Forth and Clyde Canal.

On May 20th Father received word from the police that a boy of 9 had fallen into the canal at Maryhill. He proceeded immediately to the spot and started searching. He was joined by police who searched all the waste ground and derelict buildings around in an all-out effort to find the missing boy. After seven days of constant searching Father recovered the boy's body.

1970 went on in the usual way, with case after case of the type I have so often

185

described already. Some of the cases of 1970 have already been related to you, grouped earlier on with cases of a similar nature.

In November a man was reported to have fallen into the river from the gangway of his ship, the South African-bound cargo ship *Custodian*, and drowned only hours before it was due to sail from its berth in Princes Dock. The man was carrying a chain block over his shoulders when he fell, and this caused him to sink immediately. Also, due to the high tide on which they were to sail, the gangway was at a very steep angle. Father was called in by the police, and after just over an hour's search he recovered the man's body.

BUCKINGHAM PALACE

I greatly regret that I am unable
to give you personally the award
which you have so well earned. I
now send you my congratulations
and my best wishes for your
future happiness.

Elizabeth R

Benjamin Parsonage, Esq.,
B.E.M.

CHAPTER 15

Ben Parsonage BEM

January 1st 1971 was a day that the Parsonage family will never forget. Father received a letter from Downing Street, in the last post of the year, telling him that the Queen had honoured him with the award of the British Empire Medal, and that his name would appear in the list of honours to be published the next day, January 1st. What a night of celebration that was, and the next day the first 'outsider' at our door to congratulate him was a friend of the family, a boatman from London. Glasgow newspapers are not published on January 1st, but English papers are and the friend had read about it in one of them. The family were all thrilled, none more than them and the congratulations poured in.

The presentation ceremony was held in Glasgow City Chambers at a luncheon attended by the directors of the Humane Society, city dignitaries and a small group of Father's friends and relatives. The Lord Provost, as Lord Lieutenant of the County, made the presentation of the medal on behalf of Her Majesty. As he pinned the medal on Father he said 'I am delighted to be commanded by the Queen to recognise your long years of service to the Glasgow Humane Society. You have done wonderful work for Glasgow.' The award was 'For dedicated and devoted service.'

As we had been limited in the number of guests that we were allowed to have at the BEM luncheon in the City Chambers, the family decided to hold a party for the rest of our friends in the Glasgow University Boat House, since Mother and Father had been married there. It was a wonderful night, one of the rare occasions when all the family were together. Although we were only about 150 yards from the house, Father arranged for someone to stay at the telephone, and insisted that the lifeboat with the outboard motor be brought upriver and tied up at the University steps. The Green resounded with mirth and laughter. Chief Superintendent George Birnie gave a lovely speech as self-appointed spokesman for all members of the Glasgow police force.

It was nice to see Mother and Father, who seldom had any social life, sitting surrounded by so many of their friends. It was a night the memory of which will always be with us.

County of the City of Glasgow
Office of Lieutenancy.

City Chambers.
Glasgow.

22nd March, 1971.

Benjamin Parsonage, Esq.,
Humane Society House,
Glasgow Green,
Glasgow, S.E.

Dear Mr. Parsonage,

The Lord Provost, as Lord Lieutenant, has been requested to present to you on behalf of Her Majesty The Queen the British Empire Medal which was awarded to you in the New Year Honours.

This Presentation is to be made at a Luncheon to be held in the City Chambers on Friday, 28th May, and I would appreciate your forwarding me a list of names and addresses of your own family and friends whom you would wish to be present. As accommodation is limited would you please confine your numbers to 10.

Yours sincerely,

Eric D Hamilton

Clerk of Lieutenancy.

Glasgow honours the King of the Clyde – Presentation by Lord Provost Liddell

The B.E.M. is the larger, brighter medal, the other is the Glasgow Corporation Medal with two bars.

Back to Auld Claes and Porridge

Naturally the celebrations did not interfere with the work, and Father was out on the third day of the year, searching for a man who was missing in the vicinity of the River Kelvin, and who had said that he might jump into the river. This turned out to be a hoax, as the man had gone home that night safe and well.

On February 4th at about 10.35 pm the phone rang and Father was informed that a man had jumped from the South Portland Street Suspension Bridge. We rushed downstream in the lifeboat, lifted it out and carried it round the weir as the tide was very low on the downside of the gates, continued downstream, and arrived in time to help firemen lift the body from the water.

Police had taken the ship's boat from the *Carrick* and caught hold of the half-submerged man, and firemen had thrown them ropes. Father examined the man's body which was, unfortunately, well and truly beyond help. As the tide was so low it would have been very dangerous to try to lift our boat back round the weir, so Father tied up his boat at the Clyde Trust Wharf and came down in the early hours of the morning to row it back home through the weir at tide time.

G

Hero Dived to his Death in the River

Father received word from the police around 3.30 pm, that a man had drowned in the River Clyde near Belvidere Hospital. This was a real tragedy, the man who drowned was the Scots-born son of an immigrant, Robert Mohamet, and he gave his life in an attempt to save a 3-year-old boy from drowning. Robert was working on a wall at Belvidere Hospital when he heard cries from the boy who was playing on the river bank when he slipped and fell in. Robert dived straight in and struggled to reach the boy, but couldn't make it and disappeared. The boy was rescued by two other men who arrived on the scene. Father raced to the locus and searched till well after dark, without result. Next day, Father found a pair of spectacles further down the bank, which caused him to concentrate his search down river. On the Wednesday it was established that the spectacles did not belong to Robert, and Father was also told that he could not swim. Father took all these things into account and changed the area of his search again. After about an hour's search he recovered Robert's body further upstream.

The Rowing Clubs

One aspect of living on the river that I have not really referred to is looking after the clubs. I have said that Father did not like to mention accidents involving clubs because he did not wish parents of participating youngsters to think that there was anything dangerous in the sport. Most times when Father brought out a sculler or other oarsman who had capsized they were in no danger. They were well-drilled in procedure: hanging on to their boats etc, but on quite a number of occasions there could have been a more serious ending to a matter that most of us joke about in clubs as 'a ducking' if Father hadn't acted with his usual speed. Then there were times when the oarsmen would have been perfectly safe but, having fallen in, started to panic and scream and shout, and wave their arms instead of hanging on to their boats. Anyway, I am very proud to say that in Father's 60 years on the river there never was an accident of a really serious nature involving the boat users. The letters from every club at the beginning of 1971, when Father was awarded the BEM, show the respect that they had for him: clubs did not go out on the river without his say-so, and regattas weren't run unless he gave the O.K. Sometimes he would shout and bawl at them for doing things like changing seats on the river, standing up in their boats, going too near the weir – many little points which seemed trivial to some, or which seemed as though he was trying to pick faults to others, but all of which made sport on the river safe. Oarsmen fell in while training; learners, even experienced oarsmen, ran into each other; riggers or gates breaking, 'catching crabs': endless is the list of ways that an oarsman can go for an 'early bath'!

The exact tally of oarsmen Father fished out will never be known, but over the years it amounted to a large number. I know that over the last 20 years of his life there were roughly 12 to 15 scullers per year, on average, that were glad to see Father's boat drawing alongside, and Father said that in the 1920s and 1930s dozens of scullers fell in as they were learning to scull in old-fashioned sculling boats. For those of you who are interested in rowing, this type of boat was similar to the old V-sectioned one that hangs in our boat shed, and which Father used to row.

He treated the lifting of a sculler from the water with the same urgency as any other call for help, because he never knew when a sculler or oarsman could be in real difficulty. A city lecturer tells of three 'duckings' when he was glad to see Father with his boat. Many prominent persons in Glasgow's business world, lawyers, doctors, teachers, engineers were fished out while they were members of Glasgow University. He pulled out visiting scullers from Egypt, Norway, England, members of every club: City of Glasgow, Clyde, printers', Clydesdale, Stirling, Aberdeen, Loch Lomond, Glasgow University, Glasgow Argonauts, Royal West, schoolboys and girls from Whitehill, St Mungo's, Holyrood, Hillpark, Hutcheson's, Glasgow High, Hillhead High, George Watson's, Albert, St Aloysius', Allan Glen's, Govan High, Bellahouston, Crookston Castle – the list is almost endless. One young Loch Lomond man summed it up when he said: 'We always feel safe coming to row up at the Clyde, 'cause we know you are there, Bennie. You are like a saviour to us.' We could tell that Father was proud to hear these words.

Kingston Bridge Rescue

Just into Saturday March 27th 1971, at 1.05 am to be exact, Father received a call that two persons were in the River Clyde, midstream, near to the new Kingston Bridge. A Land Rover arrived at the house within seconds, the boat trailer was hitched up, and Father and I jumped into the back. With light flashing and klaxon blaring the Land Rover drove as fast as conditions would allow down Clyde Street, towards Finnieston. As we sped down the road, ahead in the distance we saw the lights of a number of a police cars at Kingston Bridge. Father knew there was nowhere to launch the boat there, and that we would need help to launch it fast at the Finnieston Ferry steps, so as we sped past the police cars we were hanging out of the doors shouting and waving for them to follow us.

As we skidded to a halt at the ferry steps, Father and I were already halfway out to loosen the ropes holding the boat onto the trailer. The policemen leapt from

193

the cars that had followed us down, and a dozen Glasgow bobbies lifted the boat like it was made of paper, over the spiked fence at the top of the ferry steps, and launched it. With Father seated on his plank at the stern, his eyes already flashing across the river surface, picking out anything that lay on the water, I spun the bow around and sprinted out of the ferry dolphin. In my haste I snapped one of the oars in two, so I rowed out into the river with only half an oar in one hand. I still managed to go faster than the ferry that had been directed to search upriver. A third boat, manned by police, was also on the river.

Father suddenly shouted to me to head in the direction he was pointing – his hawk-like eyes had spotted the woman floating just under the surface. He lifted her into the boat and applied artificial respiration: no result; he started slapping her face and shouting at her 'What's you name? Tell me your name. Come on, speak to me.' And you could see Father's face breaking into a smile when he heard the old lady mumble 'Stop hitting me, stop hitting me.' He rolled her up in a coat, and I rowed as fast as I could to the south bank below Kingston Bridge, where we could see an ambulance. Father said she had to be taken to hospital as fast as possible, and there wasn't time to return to the ferry steps, so he placed ropes around her shoulders and threw them up onto the quay wall next to the ambulance and she was lifted out. We were told that the second person reported in the water was a man who had managed to get back out himself. We returned to Finnieston Ferry steps, where the boat was lifted out and put back onto the trailer at 1.25 am. The Chief Constable sent congratulations over the air to everyone concerned for a really slick piece of work.

The next day seemed far removed from the turmoil of the previous day's rescue. Father and I went down to Princes Dock to recover the body of a man. The boat was lowered by crane into the dock, and the body recovered. We returned home and had lunch and, since all was quiet, I decided to go for a row on the river in my sculling boat. As I reached Rutherglen Bridge I heard some shouting and, looking over my shoulder, I saw something splashing in the river near the big pipe that comes out of the banking at Strathclyde School. I sprinted to the spot and saw that it was a woman in the river, dived in and caught hold of her. She was shouting for her child, and I realised that it must be in the water. I dived and caught hold of a small bundle about 10 feet down – the child. On the surface again, I picked up the woman and swam with her and her child to the bank. Passers by lifted the woman up the bank while I gave artificial respiration to the child.

By now word had gone out to Father in the Green and he was racing to the spot. The woman and the child and I were taken to the janitor's house in Strathclyde School until the arrival of the ambulance. Father arrived and, after checking that the woman and boy were O.K. he recovered my boat and took us back home. Father was very proud of me, as I was proud of his teaching, and I was thrilled when I joined him on the list of recipients of the Corporation Medal for Bravery.

194

Bennie, George and Sarah

'You can't keep the Parsonage family out of the news. Ben has been the hero of countless rescues on the Clyde since joining the Glasgow Humane Society in 1928. And yesterday son George, 28, followed in Father's footsteps. He was awarded the Corporation Medal for Bravery and a Royal Humane Society Testimonial for saving a mother and her 5 year old son from drowning. Ben said 'It's a proud day for my wife Sarah and myself. He did a good job.' High praise indeed from a man who already has the Corporation Medal and two bars.

How many times in this book have I spoken about how fanatical Father was about not leaving things floating in the river for children to find. To emphasize why, let me tell you of the incident that Father was called to in April 1971. A boy of 8 was drowned in the canal near Firhill Football Stadium. He had been playing on the canal bank when he saw an oil drum floating in the water. He jumped on it, it turned over, hitting him on the head, and he went under the water. Father recovered the boy's body after a short search. In one week Father took two oil drums from the river that someone had thrown in, not only with disregard for the beauty of the river but with no thought for children who go down to play with such items.

Running Repairs

In August 1971, as happened so many times, Father's lifeboats were thrown into the water – three of them; one was never found, one was found smashed to pieces into the harbour and, fortunately, we found one only slightly damaged. How Father put up with this kind of thing year after year I don't know – his patience was amazing. He built his boatshed, it was washed partly away and damaged in a flood – he rebuilt it – next a gale took the roof away – he repaired it – then a gale brought a large tree crashing down, smashing the shed, the boats, wood, everything to pieces – so he cleared the area, bought another shed from the Army and cut it into sections, floated it down river to the wharf and used it to build a shed the exact same size as the one the tree destroyed – then that shed was destroyed by fire – so guess what – he rebuilt again! What fantastic perseverance: nothing ever put Father off, he took it all in his stride.

On into 1972, with recoveries like that of a boy of 7 from the Forth and Clyde Canal west of Ruchill Bridge. The same tragic circumstance again: the boy fell into the canal when he tried to reach an old ball that was floating in the water. Then Father was down again at Rothesay Dock, recovering the body of a seaman who had fallen off his ship, the Merchant Vessel *Everity*.

About 10 pm one Wednesday night in February 1972, Father was having one of his 'look-outs' from our hall window when he saw a woman climbing the fencing along the riverbank. He ran down the stairs, out of the door and down the brae to the fence where three men were standing. They had brought the woman back over the fence onto the road, but she had run off into the darkness, down towards the jail square. Father knew that if the woman really wanted to commit suicide she would simply climb the fence further downstream, so he ran off down the river bank in the direction the woman had taken, and was just in time to 'rugby tackle' her at the water's edge. He persuaded her to accompany him to the house where she was looked after until the arrival of police officers, who took her into custody 'for her own good' as she was in an unsuitable state of mind to be let loose.

On Friday February 25th 1972 at around 11.20 pm , when he was just dozing off to sleep like most people at that hour of the night, the phone rang and Father was asked to go to Princes Dock where a man had been drowned.

The boat was launched at the steps next to the 'Skye Navy's' hut on the wharf at Govan Dry Dock, and I rowed the boat, with Father in the stern making ready his equipment, up the dock to where the accident had occurred. The ship was a coastal minesweeper of the Royal Navy Volunteer Reserve, and it was a junior rating that had drowned. He had fallen between the boat and the quay wall and, after a short search, Father asked if the boat could be moved. Navy personnel scurried about and moved the ship manually to allow me to back Father's boat between the ship and the quay wall. Within a few minutes at around 3.30 am Father recovered the body directly below where the ship had been. By the time the boat had been lifted out, put back on the trailer and we had returned home, it was not worth going to bed so Mother put the kettle and the frying pan on and cracked the eggs into it, while I nipped over to the Co-op to buy a dozen freshly-baked rolls, and then the family and the policemen (who had missed their tea-break being out with us) all sat down at the fire for breakfast.

A few days later Father answered the phone and the police informed him that there was a body in the river at Finnieston. The trailer was hitched up again and the Land Rover headed down river. The body was behind the piles at the vehicular ferry, in such a position that was impossible to release it. How the body drifted there is a secret that the river holds, and the river seldom divulges its secrets. Father had to get large wooden wedges and, working from the boat with these and a large hammer, he wedged the piles away from the top of the dolphin to make a gap large enough for the body to be brought through. He dropped a grapnel to hook onto the body's clothing but this was not strong enough to hold the body, so Father and the police had to wait for the tide to rise enough for the body to be secured by reaching through the gap and lifted out.

In July 1972 I was away doing what Father would have loved to have done but never managed: racing in the Diamond Sculls at Henley royal Regatta. He was at home working as usual when at 11.30 one evening he received a call from the Police Information room that a woman had fallen from the Albert bridge into the River Clyde and disappeared. He raced down river to the weir, lifted his boat out, pulled it across the 70 to 80 yards of grass and launched it again on the downside.

Mr. Ben Parsonage, of the Glasgow Humane Society, and a
policeman search for the missing man at Albert Bridge today.

He proceeded down river looking for the woman and, at a point about ten yards east of the Victoria Bridge, he came across the woman still floating. He lifted her into his boat and was able to revive her with artificial respiration. He shouted to the police on the bank to phone for an ambulance to meet him at the Clyde Trust Wharf below Central Station railway bridge and, after making the woman as comfortable as possible, rowed there. She was taken ashore and removed to the Royal Infirmary, where she made a good recovery.

In August a watchman was found dead in a builder's yard in the Gallowgate. Murder Squad detectives led by Detective Superintendent Hugh Mackenzie, Glasgow's Deputy CID boss, went to the scene minutes after the old man was found in a pool of blood. At 11 am the following morning the Eastern CID requested that a search be made of the River Clyde. As Father was away on another case, I took CID officers out with me in one of our boats and rowed them up and down the river along the banking, looking for a blue shirt and a white pair of trousers. In the afternoon we lifted two boats around the tidal weir and searched down river to Finnieston without success. Father returned home and found part of a blue denim shirt right under our noses, on the banking just downstream of our boatshed. It was sent to the police lab and later Father had to appear in court to identify the fragment.

On a day later in August, at 4.10 am, two policemen came to our door to inform us that a man had fallen from the parapet of the Albert Bridge. Father and I pulled some clothes on and raced to the spot behind the weir, where we launched our boat. After a short search, Father recovered the body of a young man. Although he had fallen from the centre of the upstream side of the bridge with an upgoing tide, this man was recovered at the downstream side of the bridge close to the north centre pier. The tide had risen enough to allow us to bring our boat back to the wharf through the weir.

On Wednesday September 27th, 1972 at about 10 pm Father received word from Central Police that a boy of 3 had fallen into the Clyde near Customs House Quay.

Father and I took the boat by Land Rover to the back of the Tidal Weir. The tide being one of the lowest, we had a terribly difficult job putting the boat into the water. I had never seen the water so low at the back of the weir – there were large rocks and areas of shingle everywhere I looked. Wooden posts jutted out above the water and others were just below the surface, just showing as the current rippled over them. It was amazing how Father knew every shallow and channel and was able to guide the boat slowly down river. We arrived at the spot about halfway between the South Portland Street Suspension Bridge and the Jamaica Bridge on the north bank, to be told that two children of 6 and 7 had seen a child of 3 fall into the water and sink. Father thought it unlikely that a child so small would sink immediately and, since there was a fairly strong current running, we rowed downstream to Finnieston Ferry, searching every corner of the river in case the child had floated down. Back at the quay without success, Father commenced dragging.

After a while the two witnesses arrived along with Detectives Joyce and Sloan. The children now said that the child had been last seen floating arms outstretched, face down, out into the middle of the river. Father had a conference on the quay wall with the detectives and then in the Central Police Office, with Detectives Dalgleish and Beattie. He decided that if the child had floated out (though he thought it unlikely with the state of the tide) it could have drifted for miles.

Father arranged for a policeman to accompany us in the boat, equipped with both a Central and a Marine walkie-talkie and heavy-duty flashlamps. Using our heavy outboard engine, we searched every inch of the river in an effort to make sure the child wasn't floating around. This took until 5 am, when we came home, and after about three hours sleep Father returned to the search and I went to school.

From Thursday September 28th the search continued, until Tuesday October 3rd, when Father attended the High Court for the trial of the man accused with the watchman's murder, to identify the shirt that he had found on the river bank. Then on Wednesday October 4th Father recovered the boy's body one and a half miles down river at Stobcross Quay. The Assistant Chief Constable's letter (11th October 1972) describes the manner of the body's recovery:

Dear Sir,

I wish to bring to your notice the commendable actions of Mr. Ben Parsonage, care of the Glasgow Humane Society, Glasgow Green, Glasgow, in recovering the body of a three year old boy from the River Clyde at Stobcross Quay on Wednesday, 4th October, 1972.

The services of Mr. Parsonage were requested on Wednesday, 27th September, 1972 after the child had fallen into the River from Customs House Quay at a point east of Jamaica Bridge, and he displayed his usual patient determination when he dragged the water between Customs House Quay and King George V Bridge on 27th, 28th, 29th and 30th September, a total of 36 hours on the River. No trace was found of the child's body and Mr. Parsonage from his experience and knowledge of the River was of the opinion that it would surface about 4th or 5th October at or near Finnieston Quay.

About 9 am on Wednesday, 4th October, the body surfaced at Stobcross Quay and Mr. Parsonage again provided valuable assistance in its recovery. In order to effect this recovery Mr. Parsonage descended a rope ladder between the quay side and the side of a vessel moored there, and having positioned himself on a floating baulk of timber succeeded in affixing the line to the body enabling it to be removed. Due to turbulence in the River caused by a passing vessel Mr. Parsonage for a time was placed in considerable danger.

The praiseworthy determined efforts of Mr. Parsonage are much appreciated by the Police Service in this City and I shall be obliged if you will convey my sincere thanks to him for his co-operation on this occasion.

The following letter is from the Co-operative Bakery in McNeill Street, Glasgow, our nearest neighbours for many years. Every 'Co-op' man got to know Father during their dinner hours, as they would come and sit by the boats talking to him, and in the early boat-hiring days the Co-op lads and lassies hired boats. The men on the night shift saw Father most nights, when he would go for his last check on the lifeboats and the river before turning in for the night, and sometimes when he would return home from a case in the early hours of the morning, Mother would put the frying pan on, Father would cross the bridge and buy piping-hot rolls from the 'Co' – and he and the policemen would sit down and have a meal.

At New Year, Father and I would cross the river to wish the Co-op gatemen a Happy New Year. The gatemen knew the whole family, as the gatehouse was a stopping place from which we were all escorted by Father, or by some friend if he was away on a case, across the bridge, as Father would let none of us cross the Green alone. It is very sad to see this traditional Glasgow bakery now closed.

To the Treasurer, Glasgow Humane Society,

Dear Sir,
We have pleasure in enclosing cheque for £22.50 being donation from the above society. It is regretted that this will be our last contribution to the funds of your organisation as our Society is now being wound up.

From the Co-operative Shareholding Society Ltd.,
12 McNeill Street, Glasgow C5.

CHAPTER 16
Troubled Waters

The first few weeks of 1973 found oil floating down the river—heavy thick oil like tar, the type that we learned to hate, that Father saw so often over the years. It floats just on the surface, and when it comes downriver at first you hardly notice it, and this was the case the day that one of my clubmates and I were out sculling and ran into one of these patches of oil and were held tight as though our boats were on a large sucker. Well, there I was, well and truly stuck. Any move could easily have caused me to fall into the oil, and that would have been a terrible fate. My clubmate was in a similar position, so we held our frail boats as steady as we could, and shouted to people on the bank to 'get Bennie'. Father arrived and had to 'cut' us free: he had to prize the oil away from our boats carefully, everything was covered in it, the boat surfaces were ruined, our clothes were ruined, but I think we were lucky to be able to return to the club in the condition we did. The smell of the oil is terrible, you can't rid yourself of it, it hangs around you, you feel it, hate it, you never really clean it from the boats, and you have to burn your clothes, the oil stays around the river for years after the spillage. It sticks to the grass at the water's edge, it claims the lives of pigeons, seagulls, ducks and swans: you can't let anyone out in a boat, because the least splash of water could put oil on their clothes. We respect the river, fear the weir, its currents and floods, but we loathe the oil, hate it, it is a disgusting substance.

Often there was no good reason for it being on the water. 'Regrettable incidents' would occur, usually during the Glasgow Fair holidays or Christmas and Easter holidays, when the big works were closed down and were taking the chance to clean our their tanks, and it seemed that instead of cleaning them properly they just let the oil flow into the river, although that was seldom proven.

You never knew when it was coming down, so you hadn't time to lift the boats out before it arrived, so Father's boats and barges would get covered in oil. When I was young I remember the oil being trapped feet thick at the weir, and to stop it going into the harbour, attempts were made to lift it out. Corporation bosses, Cleansing, Purification, labourers—all turned up at the weir, the oil was scooped into drums, loaded onto lorries and taken away. Father's barges were already covered in oil, so the two similar ones (about 20 feet by 15 feet) were towed down to the weir and used as platforms for the oil lifting. Hoses sprayed some emulsifying agent onto it, which helped a bit, but not much. When the work was finished the barges were lifted out onto the banking behind our shed, but nothing could be done to clean them and Father finally burned them—a terrible loss.

Sad as it is to see the big oil-using industries upriver closing down, these closures are the best thing that has happened in terms of cleaning up of the river. I would have dearly loved to have shoved one of the bosses of one of the guilty firms into the oil-covered river, but Father would never have let me, and anyway, the smell was so bad I doubt that a boss would ever have gone near enough the water!

A man from the Health Board who used to walk through the Park said he was amazed that Father's health didn't suffer terribly from the filthy conditions he worked in. I will never forget the oil, it has left me with such a hate for that smell that even writing about it brings the memory back as though it was still there.

Ice

Talking about the oil reminds me of the time there was ice on the river. It must have been in the early 60's during a really cold spell. There had been a thaw and large trees and ice were coming down the river. some of the trees were so big that they jammed right across the 40 feet of the weir gate, pier to pier, and with ice piling up and up on top of the trees the weir gates could not be lifted clear. This is a very dangerous situation, for during heavy runs the weir gates are lifted to let all the rubbish flow unhindered right down the river.

With the weir jammed, the City Engineers rushed down to the Green with truckloads of workers to see what they could do. Father was asked to help, and I rowed him downriver to the scene. As usual we approached the weir with caution, but as I tried to back the stern of the boat down beside the logs, the ice whipped at my oars and smashed the blades to pieces. We threw a rope as fast as possible to the bank, and workmen took the strain, keeping the bow of the boat upstream. Had our boat turned side-on to the gate then I might not be writing this story. The water was surging through the trees, over and under the weir gate, and the ice was crashing against the planks of the boat, as though it would break it to pieces.

Father climbed onto one of the big trees, put ropes around it, and threw them up to the waiting men on the top of the weir and the tree was lifted from the water. Another rope was thrown to the bank and the tree was pulled onto the banking to be cut up and removed. This procedure was repeated until the gate was clear enough to allow it to be lifted. Mr Riddit, the City Engineer, said that Father did the work of ten men that night, and I can certainly verify that.

Tragedy

Wednesday June 27th, 1973 brought real tragedy to the river. Earlier I related the sad story of the man Robert Mohamet who gave his life in an attempt to save a young boy from drowning (the boy was rescued by others). This Wednesday it wasn't a young boy who fell in, it was a man.

When Police Constable Colin MacDuff arrived on the quay wall he saw only a man in the water, another human in distress and immediately dived to the rescue, a true hero's action. Colin MacDuff did not know that this was a man who would later be charged in court with attempting to commit suicide. What a cruel quirk of fate: the man was saved, but Colin MacDuff was drowned. Father recovered the policeman's body after about an hour's search.

The following statement was issued:

> The Police Constable who died was 28 years old Colin MacDuff. He had served with the Glasgow force for the past 5 years and received a commendation for brave conduct. He drowned while trying to save a man who plunged into the river from the parapet of the bridge.

One of the witnesses told his story to a newspaper:

> When I looked over I saw a policeman swimming towards a man in the water. He had almost reached him when suddenly the P. C. went under, resurfaced then went under again and never reappeared.
> The young man in the water was brought out safely but it was an hour before the body of Constable MacDuff was recovered by Mr Ben Parsonage. The spot where the Constable disappeared was 18 feet deep. A report of the incident has been sent to the city's procurator fiscal.

Later in the year the papers reported:

> 3 MONTHS FOR MAN P. C. DIED TRYING TO RESCUE.
> A young policeman drowned rescuing a man trying to kill himself in the river. Said Sheriff Middleton, 'I do not regard it as a serious attempt at suicide but it had tragic consequences.'

On Friday 6th July at about 4.40 pm a police car arrived at the boatshed and enquired if we knew anything about a man being attacked near our house. We did not, but while we were talking a man came up with his face all bloody and said he had been beaten up. He had a good drink in him. Father recognised him having been with a woman of dubious character a short time previously. This indeed was what had happened: he had gone down to the river with this woman when two men had set upon him, robbed him of his wallet and watch, and taken his spectacles. We found his spectacles on the bank later that evening.

Later, at about 10 pm, Father and I searched the banks of the Clyde downstream of the weir on the north bank, at the request of the Central police— I was never told what we were looking for. Father and the CID had a long chat about the search, but to this day I do not know what was involved.

On Sunday July 8th 1973 at 12.30 am Father received a report of a woman in the river at Clyde Street. He rushed to the scene and found that a young woman had been seen acting oddly on the walkway and later her handbag had been found on the ledge overlooking the water. Unfortunately there were no witnesses as to where the woman had actually jumped in. Father started searching but we weren't able to stay there long, for at 2.45 am, Father received word that there had been an accident at Princes Dock.

Since it would have taken much longer to lift the boat out and convey it by road, we just rowed the two miles to Princes Dock. When we arrived we found that a watchman had fallen between his ship and the quay wall. Father recovered the body after a few minutes. The CID were sent for, as there seemed to be some suspicious circumstances in this drowning. After a thorough examination, these suspicions were allayed, and Father and the police doctor had a long talk before we returned home.

At 10.15am the following Thursday Father recovered the body of the young woman who had drowned at the suspension bridge on July 8th at Finnieston Ferry. The CID came to the scene to examine some suspicious marks that Father had noticed on the woman's body.

In September 1973 a policeman came running to the door at 9.15 pm to inform Father that a woman was in the river at Stockwell bridge. The trailer was hooked to the Land Rover and we sped to behind the weir, where the boat was launched and we proceeded downstream:

Father caught sight of the woman , floating head down just under the surface. She was lifted into the boat and rushed to the Clyde Trust wharf, artificial respiration being applied the whole way. Father said that the woman had been under the water for too long, and this was confirmed after a police car had raced her to the Royal Infirmary (the ambulance drivers were on strike).

October 1973 brought another case where Father's knowledge gained over the years was put to good use. Around 4.40 pm he was called by the Central police to the River Clyde at Queen's Dock. As he approached the body, he realised that it had only been in the water for a relatively short time, and if he didn't get hold of it immediately it would sink. He caught it with his boat-hook and then his hands, and quickly tied it up. He rowed the boat back to the Finnieston ferry steps where he had launched, and boat and body were lifted out. Father thought the man had been in the water for about eight hours.

One November night in 1973 at 11.45 pm a Land Rover arrived outside the house and a policeman came to the door to take Father to the new walkway on Clyde Street, where there was a report of a body being in the river.

The body had sunk by now, but after a few minutes' search, Father recovered the young man's body. Just after midnight the CID arrived to inspect the body, as Father had noticed some suspicious circumstances about the drowning.

The year finished with Father locating the body of a man at the tidal weir on December 30th.

Early in 1974 Father and I launched a boat at Finnieston Ferry and, with a policeman equipped with a walkie-talkie on board, proceeded downriver into Queen's Dock. Father had been asked to attend at the dock by the police after a report of a body in the water there. The body was lying in the middle of a lot of heavy rubbish, and large wooden fenders with ropes. The ropes strung from the quay wall to the fenders wrapped around the body. Father found that he could not move the body from the rubbish because of these large ropes. Up on the quay wall along with the police was a fire engine. Father shouted up for an axe to be passed down, but even better, large sharp knifes were produced from the fire boat which lay nearby. He cut the body free and we towed it back to the ferry steps. The CID were in attendance because the body was all tied up, and they took photographs before it was removed to the mortuary. The body was badly decomposed and Father thought that the ropes had been twisted round it by the movement of the currents.

The year continued with the treatment of youngsters who injured themselves in the park, the recovery of bodies from the Clyde and the canal, people again trying to steal our lifeboats, a man falling off a motor boat and incidents like the following.

One morning, when he was out on the river, Father noticed boxes lying at the side of the river below the Gorbals skyscrapers. On inspection, he found they contained drugs. He sent for the police who, finding they were dangerous, started a search of the area and warned people to hand over any drugs they found immediately.

It was around this time, the sewage works being on strike , that Father had to advise the Glasgow schools to stay off the river.

At 4.15 pm on October 14th 1974 Father received word from Easterhouse police that a patient was missing from the hospital at Gartcosh. He went to inspect the area around the Bishop Loch to see if it was possible to launch a boat. After a thorough search it was decided to try next to the farm on the opposite bank from the hospital.

Father arranged for a Land Rover to come at 9 am to pick him up. He also took note of a small pond which police had searched on the Sunday. He searched all around the perimeter with the Support Unit. In the afternoon we searched the same area again and also the small pond. Reports of sightings of a man answering the description were coming in from Glasgow to Dumfries. We returned home leaving the police Dog Branch and the Mounted Branch to continue the search.

The Bishop Loch proved to be only 18 inches to 2 feet deep at the deepest, and it would have needed someone of great strength and will power to wade through the marshland to even reach the loch. The man turned up later alive and well.

Low Water

If you look at the river banks opposite our boatshed you will see that they have sunk several feet—that happened when the water level fell too low in the 1920's. Further down the bank you can see where the walkway and pavement in front of the skyscrapers has collapsed and also above the suspension bridge on the north bank, cracks like a miniature earthquake can be seen on the banks and the Glasgow schools' boathouses have moved several inches from their original positions. This happened when the water fell too low in the early 1970's. Almost the same happened again in 1974, and I am amazed that so important a feature as the tidal weir does not have an emergency generator for use in the event of power failure.

On Saturday November 10th, 1974 at about 11.30 pm, Father and I rushed down to the wharf when we noticed from the house window that the river level seemed very low. Indeed it was almost at danger level, with land showing almost up to the edge of our wharf.

Continuous telephoning to the weir produced only the engaged tone. We phoned to ask the Southern police to hurry down to the weir to make sure the weirman was all right. We then phoned the Eastern Division to ask if we could have transport to take Father and myself to the weir. When we arrived an Inspector from the Southern Division was with the weirman. It seemed that there was a power failure and the electricity on the weir was out. The weirman had been on the phone constantly trying to telephone his bosses. Inspector Turner, the weirman, the two Eastern policemen, Father and I had to put the gates down manually to stop the water falling further and causing real damage.

Helping to put the weir gates down by hand was worse than any circuit training I have done over the years. The sweat poured out of the policeman, the weirman, Father and I as we took it in turns to wind the large metal handles, like giant starting-handles. My back was breaking, and I'm meant to be at least semi-fit, and goodness knows how the policeman felt. As for Father—well he was so strong, and he never complained. It was really good to see the Police Inspector setting an example, showing his men how to work.

Just afterwards power was returned to the weir. It was most fortunate that we

207

had noticed this and that there had been police available to help, as goodness knows what would have happened had the water fallen further.

The weir gates have jammed open several times—in 1975, 1976, in June 1977, and again in July 1977, when Father and police had a terrible job lifting lifeboats from the water where they were about to be smashed by the falling water but, fortunately, prompt action has prevented more serious incidents.

At 3 pm one blustery, cold January afternoon in 1975 Father received word that a man had been seen in the River Clyde near Balmoral Street, Scotstoun. He proceeded there to recover the body. There was no spot in the vicinity where Father could launch his boat, so one of the dockside cranes was used to lower him and his boat into the water. The body was tied up very carefully and lifted out, along with the boat by crane. The tide was low and there was much more soft mud out from the quay wall than usual. It's not often that Father used a crane to lift a body out, but, as I say, things never happen in ones — so the following occurred.

On Tuesday, January 28th, 1975 at about 2.00 pm the doorbell rang. It was two policemen who asked Father if he could go with them to assist in the recovery of the body of a woman from the River Clyde at the Broomielaw. The trailer was hitched up immediately, and the boat towed to the police patrol boat wharf where it was launched..

Father rowed downriver to the spot, only to find that it was impossible to get to the body because it was behind the piles being sunk for the new walkway. The police launch was at the spot, but could do nothing as they also had no way of getting to the body. Father rowed back to the police wharf, the boat was lifted out and taken by road to the spot on the quay wall above the body. Father and the boat were lowered by a crane into the space between the piles and the quay wall. He tied up the body which was lifted out by the crane. The boat and Father were in turn lifted out, and both returned home. The body, that of a fairly young woman, was in a terribly decomposed state.

In February 1975 Father was called to Princes Dock by the Govan Police to search for a man missing from the crew of the tug 'Wrestler'. The missing man had been with a woman who had subsequently been arrested. Father viewed the scene, but on police advice decided to wait till next morning in the hope that the man would turn up safe and well.

He searched for several days around the dock as tugs came and went. At the opposite quay wall, gun boats of the Mexican Navy were tied up, and the sailors lined the decks, watching. These small ships had been built at Yarrows, and their crews were being shown how to use them in preparation for their voyage to America.

Father had to spend some time away from Princes Dock when a man was seen to fall from the George V Bridge, another man was drowned in a canal, and another drowned at Clyde Bridge, so it wasn't until a few weeks later that the body of the man was recovered in Princes Dock.

On Sunday March 30th at 6.55 am we received a telephone call from the Tidal Weir that the weirman had seen what he thought was a body at the centre gate. Father and I rushed there immediately. The body was lying balanced over the gate on the small of its back. Father tied the body up in the usual manner, but could not move the body off the gate. The weirman lowered the gate as far as he could into the water but still the body would not move from its precarious position. The weirman lowered a rope which Father fastened to the body enabling him to lift it a little while Father and I levered the body off the gate. The body was later brought to our wharf to await the arrival of the shell (temporary coffin).

On Monday March 31st 1975, at about 8.30 pm, Father received word from the Govan Police that there was the body of a man lying on the steps at the Govan Ferry. We rushed to Stag Street, where we launched the boat and went downriver to the locus. We landed next to the body and Father tied it up. The bank was very slippery and was all loose boulders, so it was with great difficulty that we managed to get the body back into the river as a very high fence prevented it from being lifted at that spot. We towed the body up to the Stag Street Ferry where we landed it. The boat was lifted out at the mouth of Princes Dock. This also was very difficult, as the water had fallen 4 or 5 feet below the bottom of the steps.

One morning in May, Father was having his pre-breakfast look around the boatsheds to make sure that all was well when he saw a coat lying over the railing near the suspension bridge. Father was always suspicious of things like this, and searched along the river bank, where he found the body of a man lying in shallow water. He took the body to the Humane Society's wharf and phoned the police who came and had the body removed to the City Mortuary.

On Friday May 30th 1975 at about 3.45 pm Father received word from the police in Govan that there was a woman missing from the Govan area whose handbag containing a suicide note had been found beside the Bishop Loch in Easterhouse, and it was assumed she had drowned herself in the loch. We proceeded there with the boat. We searched the weeds and bullrushes by wading, then put the boat into the loch and continued the search further out into the centre. After about an hour, Father recovered the body of the woman in the rushes. She had been in the water for some time but was hidden from view by the height of the bullrushes.

Scrap

When Father searched the canal at the rear of the White House pub in Maryhill Road for the body of a young man who had been drowned, he lifted so much rubbish from the canal that the police said they should have asked a scrap merchant to attend. This happened so often over the years that Father's friends, and the police who watched him dragging, said he could have made his fortune in scrap! Certainly, those who clean up the canal now would have been proud of him. The man's body was finally recovered.

On Friday October 10th 1975 at 4.20 pm Father received word that there was a body floating in the river at the Albert Bridge. Father and I went downstream through the weir, where we met the police patrol boat coming upstream. We both searched the area but could find nothing. It seemed that someone had made a mistake, so the patrol boat went off to tie up and go home.

Father had me row alongside the quayside so that he could have a talk with the Inspector. It was then that the Inspector told Father that there had been a bad mistake in the reports. It was not a floating body that we had been called out for, but one of the painters on the Albert Bridge had fallen from the top of the ladder which went from the parapet down to the scaffolding planks into the water and drowned. He did not have his life jacket on when he fell in. Twice that evening Father tried to make a search, but he couldn't because of the high, stormy water and the terrible flooding. The following morning, Father recovered the body of the painter west of the Albert Bridge, in line with the ladder.

One day in December , Father and I noticed a man trying to climb the parapet of the suspension bridge outside our house. We rushed onto the bridge and caught hold of him. Three times, when we seemed to have quietened him down and ceased to hold him tightly, he tried to throw himself in, but we restrained him. He was in a terrible state, but Father managed to sit talking to him quietly until the police arrived, and on Father's advice he was taken into custody for his own good.

Some days later a similar incident occurred: a man started acting daft on the suspension bridge. Father said not to go rushing towards him, as that might cause him to jump. My sister phoned the police, and I went down and sat in the lifeboat while Father sauntered up onto the bridge.

When he saw Father close to him, he moved off up McNeill Street. When the police arrived, Father told them that the man seemed 'high' on drugs. They went after him and removed him to hospital.

Vandals

1976 started in a way none of us wanted. At 3 am on January 2nd Father received word from the weirman that there were two boats at the north gate of the tidal weir. We rushed down to our wharf to find that two of Father's lifeboats that he had just finished repairing and revarnishing had been thrown into the water from the top of our quay, and oars were missing from the lifeboat in the river. At the weir, one boat was upside down against the gate, and we had a very tricky job getting it righted and away from the gate as the river was in heavy spate and surging up and down. We returned home with the boats, which had been damaged, and later that morning notified the police.

On Wednesday March 3rd 1976, at about 11.30 pm, while going upstairs to bed, I saw a young man climb over the fence from the boats.

Father telephoned the police and informed them we had an intruder, and that he and I were going to investigate. A police car arrived almost immediately, and set off again in the direction the person had vanished. The lifeboat had been interfered with, but no damage had been inflicted.

The police returned with the youth who had been returning from a football match, half-drunk, and thought that he would go for a sail in the motor boat. He couldn't start the engine and, coming out of the boat, had fallen into the river. Fortunately he got out without help. He was informed that he could have lost his own life, caused someone else to lose their life in trying to help him, or caused someone else to drown if he had taken the lifeboat away. Since he had obviously got a real taste of 'poetic justice' he was not charged, and the police drove him home.

Father received word that a boy had been drowned in the Black Cart. A Land Rover arrived and we went to the spot with haste. We had difficulty in getting to the locus as there was a football match at Ibrox. We had to go up roads on the right hand side , and up central reservations with emergency lights on and the klaxon blaring.

We arrived as dusk was falling , and launched the boat. Father picked up the boy's body, lying under the water about a quarter of a mile from where he went in. The body was covered with an emergency blanket, the casualty surgeon arrived and verified death, our boat was put back on the trailer, and we returned home.

In May, Father had to go upriver to Belvidere, where the body of a man had been seen lying in the water. He lifted the man into our boat and brought him to the Humane Society Wharf. The man had not been long in the water, and Father asked the CID to attend as the man had a cut in his head which was bleeding heavily. This was later presumed to have happened when the man fell down the banking.

Father went to the canal at the request of the Marine CID to recover a handbag which had been thrown into the water after a theft from an old lady. Another day he had to go downriver to the bank at Adelphi School to examine clothing found there, and again downriver to recover a stolen brief case.

September Flood

On Tuesday September 28th 1976 terrible, torrential rain kept falling. We lifted all the boats except our number one lifeboat out of the river.

After a difficult and sometimes dangerous operation the body was recovered

At about 7 pm Father received a call from police that he was needed to rescue people trapped in their houses in Rutherglen. We proceeded there with difficulty, because of all-over flooding. After Rutherglen, we were asked to go to Springburn to rescue folk from a bus, then to Aikenhead Road for people trapped on another. In case of more accidents we stood by at the Eastern Police Headquarters.

We were asked to return to Hawthorn Street, Springburn, as a breakdown van had been flooded, along with a bus. The conditions were so bad that on the way to Springburn , the Land Rover was flooded. Using a relief Land Rover, we arrived at Springburn, and Father and I rescued the driver of the breakdown van from the roof of his vehicle and four persons from the bus. We then rushed to Meadowpark Street, Dennistoun to take persons from their flooded houses.

At about midnight we were asked by the Social Work Department to go to Carnwadric to take people from waterlogged houses.

Newspapers naturally gave coverage of these floodings:

'Glasgow goes under freak floods'

'Deluge cripples city services'

'The city was deluged by three and a half inches of rain in four hours, the heaviest concentration since the records started in 1888'

'September in the rain'

'10 feet floods rip through Glasgow'

'Ben Parsonage was called out with his boat to ferry 20 families to safety'

'5 people were taken to hospital after a bus was trapped by floodwater in Springburn'

'Mop-up after the £1m Deluge'

'The evening cruise to King's Park'

'The day that the rain came down'

'Take to the boats'

Glasgow finally dried out and things returned to 'normal'. One day Father was approached about the chance of getting a boat on the river by a young man obviously high on either drink or drugs. Father was suspicious of the man's intentions, and watched him as he ran off down the road. He climbed the fence on to the river bank, and was peeping at Father from behind the other boatshed like a child. Father phoned the police, then chased the man out onto the road. The man ran down the road, then climbed back on to the banks. The police arrived and gave Father a hand to remove the man from his position, huddled near the water's edge. He was taken into care.

One November Sunday, at about 11 am Father received word from the police that there was a body of a woman in the River Clyde at Springfield Quay. We went there immediately with the sirens blaring, because it was feared that the body would be washed away as there was a large liner coming upriver.

We launched the boat at the ferry steps, and rowed round to the body. Father fastened it up as best he could, owing to its very bad condition. He then wrapped the remains in a plastic sheet. It was so badly mangled, although having only been about three weeks in the water, it was thought that the iron ore boat had sat on top of it at low tide, squashing it flat and disfiguring it terribly.

On Thursday December 2nd at 11.45 pm the phone rang and Father was told that there was a man in the River Clyde at Mavisbank Quay. A Land Rover arrived immediately, and we heard over the wireless that the man was still alive. With siren blaring and light flashing we were sped to Mavisbank. A police car joined us, escorted us through traffic lights, and led the way into Princes Dock.

The man was in the water at the bow of a tug, and a policewoman was hanging over the quay wall shouting at him to keep moving.

There was no time to launch the boat. A rope was fastened around my waist and, with Father holding it helped by policemen, I was lowered down the quay wall, beside the man, half-in, half-out of the water. I steadied myself on a baulk of timber—a fender used for the boats—and, under Father's instructions, tied the man up so that he could be lifted. I kept talking to the man, who was near collapse; his name was Joe. Father shouted instructions to the police officer and together they lifted Joe slowly up the quay wall. I followed him up. Father and a policeman walked him to the ambulance to get some circulation and some heat into his body. We phoned home at 12.15 am to let Mother know we were both OK.

We went to Govan to get cleaned up, as I was partly soaking wet, and partly covered in thick oil from the river. My clothes had to be burned. I remember the Inspector asking why I went down the quay wall instead of Father and I informed him that I knew I was safe with Father holding the ropes and directing my movements: no one else could have. Yes, Father was the gaffer, and I shall never really feel safe without his guiding hand.

The year went out none too peacefully too. At 4 pm on Hogmanay, Father received a call from Clydebank police that there was a body in the hold of a hopper in Rothesay Dock.

We proceeded to the spot as fast as possible so we would be able to see the spot before darkness fell. The body was lying face-down in the thick muddy water. It was uplifted, with great difficulty as the man's coat was up over his head and arms, onto the walkway of the hopper, and then by ropes onto the quay wall. The man had not been long in the water. We returned home to clean ourselves up for the New Year.

1977

Into 1977 the work went on with searches at Rosebank, the canal at Maryhill, the Kelvin and, of course, the Clyde.

While out sculling one day, I noticed the body of a man hanging spreadeagled across the branches of a tree, just above Rutherglen Bridge and about 8 feet above the water. I rushed downriver and informed Father. The body must have been left there by the high tide of the previous day and it seemed amazing that none of the other river users had seen it.

Father and I had to cut branches to loosen the body from the trees and allow us to lower it into the water. It was quite horrible and frightening working with the decomposed body hanging above us, its bloated face staring wildly down, but, at last freed from its temporary resting place, the body was roped up and towed down to our wharf where the police took over.

Early in the morning , Father was searching around the Tidal Weir as there was someone missing from Dalmarnock. After breakfast as we were making ready to continue the search, the phone rang, and when my sister Elizabeth answered it we all heard the voice at the other end as it shouted, 'There's a man in the river at the weir.' We raced to the lifeboat and rushed downriver, where a man was floundering in the water on the south side. Father caught hold of him and we lifted him into the boat. While I birled the boat around and headed back to the wharf, Father was attending to the man. He lapsed into unconsciousness and Father had to bring him round. We reached the wharf and enlisted the help of a passerby to half-carry, half-walk the man to our house, where we put him to bed in our treatment room, stripped, dried, and looked after him. An ambulance and the police arrived and the man was removed to hospital, where he was detained for observation.

We set out once more for Dalmarnock but were again interrupted by having to stop at Richmond Park to chase away boys who were building a raft, and to break up the raft and dispose of it.

A few days later, Father was again en route for Dalmarnock when the phone rang and Mother was told that there was the body of a man in the river, between a boat and the quay wall, at the Iron Ore Terminal.

I drove up the river bank to return Father to the wharf in time to meet the police Land Rover. Father launched his boat at Finnieston and rowed around the bow of the ship to where the body was. He tied it up and had it lifted out, and the CID took over.

Later in the month when Father recovered a body at the Tidal Weir, the current was so heavy that it took over one hour to cover the quarter mile back to the wharf.

At 2.35 am on June 9th 1977 we were awakened from our sleep by the telephone. A woman was in the Clyde at the Albert Bridge. We pulled some clothes on and opened the gates in time to meet the Land Rover. The boat was launched behind the weir and we rowed downstream to find the woman floating on her back, her head under the water. Father caught hold of her and lifted her into the boat where he tried to resuscitate her while I rowed to the side, where an ambulance was waiting, but she was beyond help.

About 10 am one July day in 1977, two detectives came to visit Father. They wanted some information regarding a possible murder, and there was a possibility that a body was in the river. While they were sitting talking, the phone rang and Father was asked to go to the Kingston Bridge where there had been an accident, a lorry having crashed on the bridge. The driver had been killed and a taxi driver had thought that he saw what could have been a person thrown from the lorry, falling towards the river.

A Land Rover took Father and myself to the back of the weir, where we launched the boat and proceeded downriver. The weather was so rough that the waves were breaking over the boat. We could only find a police parking beacon and a welder's glove, floating in the water. We climbed onto the quay wall and phoned the police up on the bridge. They were still trying to find out if there had been anyone else in the cab. We took a policeman with us in the boat so that we could hear any messages over his radio, and searched upriver again as the tide was rising fast with the following wind.

While we were searching we received a message that there had been no one else in the lorry. Perhaps it was the large welder's glove which had been seen falling from the bridge, so we returned home.

Early one morning I saw a man inside the bank of the river acting strangely. I approached slowly and engaged him in conversation. He was in a bit of a state and contemplating suicide, but after having poured his troubles out he obviously felt better and, since he had ran out of the house without any money, I gave him his bus fare home and saw him out of the park. I have heard how Father took this sort of action many times over the years, but this was my first experience. Father never made any note of these happenings so we have no idea of how many such incidents occurred.

Another type of case that happened over the years but was seldom mentioned, were the incidents when Father was summoned as someone was in the water in danger of drowning , but they were rescued before he arrived; some of these incidents were almost as hazardous as actual rescues, but naturally the credit would go to the person or persons doing the rescue, and Father, sometimes only yards away, would slip home quietly and happy, like the night the phone rang at 12.55 am and the Control told Father that a man had jumped into the river at the walkway on Clyde Street. Throwing on a pair of trousers, Father raced back to the weir and, with great difficulty due to the lowness of the tide and the currents, launched the boat.

While rowing as fast as he could through the rocks and broken piles to the spot he received word that the man had managed to get out OK. The boat was lifted up the sloping bank and tied back onto the trailer, brought back to the house, the double gates opened and the boat trailer placed back again in its position of readiness. As I said this happened often but Father was naturally only too happy that a life had been saved.

One evening Father received word from the Maryhill Police that there was the body of a man in the canal at Maryhill near to the Hallowe'en Pen. We proceeded there immediately and launched the boat. The man's body was lifted into the boat and landed on the bank next to the police cars. Father said the body had only been in the water for about 8 to 10 hours. The casualty surgeon was sent for, and he verified that the man had not been dead for more than 24 hours, and maybe a lot less. When the man was identified, it was said that he had previously slept on the canal bank at night. It was presumed that on this occasion he had slept the night on the bank, then in the morning staggered into the canal. I was fascinated, standing on the canal bank listening to Father explaining to the relatively new casualty surgeon why he had known that the man had been in the water such short time, and pointing out the tell-tale marks, and I was proud to see how attentive the casualty surgeon was.

At about 10 am on September 17th, Father received word that clothes had been found on the banks of the Clyde at Belvidere. We went upriver in the motor launch. At a point about 100 yards west of the Rutherglen Industrial Estate on the south bank we found the woman's coat (this was 1.5 miles from Belvidere). He searched the area where the clothes had been found until the 25th of the month when he recovered the woman's body. From the way he caught hold of her, Father said that she must have been standing upright on the bed of the river. We lifted her into our boat and brought her downriver to the wharf. The CID were sent for and, after a brief examination, the body was removed to the mortuary.

The Shettleston Flood

One Friday afternoon in October 1977, at around 3.20 pm, Father was asked to attend at Shettleston, Duke Street and Rigby Street, where the roads were flooded. Father and I raced in a Land Rover to the spot. Two buses were trapped in rising water. The fire brigade had a rubber dinghy and we started ferrying the stranded passengers to safety.

The place was in chaos: vans, buses, cars, people stranded at their work.

Another bus got trapped , so Father sent me back to get another boat. While I was away, Father continued ferrying . One old woman had a heart attack on the bus, and Father had to rush her carefully to a waiting ambulance. I returned and we finished getting the people off the buses: over 100 in all.

People were still working in their offices thinking they would be all right; Father informed them that they should leave as the water would rise, and asked each of the bosses to round up their workers. Load after load of passengers was ferried to dry land. We were soaked to the skin, up to our waists in water.

Some of it was funny: bosses with their trousers rolled up to their knees, but still carrying umbrellas; The drunk who passed his bottle of Eldorado round his fellow passengers in the boat while singing 'O sole mio'.

We finally returned home with our boats, tired and wet, to find the Clyde a raging torrent. Father advised the City of Glasgow Rowing Club officials to cancel their regatta scheduled for the next day. We lifted all the lifeboats out of the water and placed them in readiness on rollers on our barge. This was only the second time I remember the floods being so bad that Father ordered all the lifeboats to be lifted.

On the last weekend in October Father recovered the body of a man from the River Clyde at the Kingston Bridge. This man had only been in the river a very short time. Then he headed for the River Kelvin as Police Control had called him because there was a woman's body in the water. The body was under a waterfall, and was bobbing up and down in the surging water, so Father had an extremely difficult job getting hold of her.

October finished with another terrible flood on the river. The Clyde was again a raging torrent. Boats were lifted from their moorings at Rutherglen, swept downriver and smashed at the weir. We were lucky: Father had anticipated the flood, all but the lifeboats were lifted out, these and the barges were firmly fastened with extra ropes and we sat up all night watching. Flooding again occurred all over Glasgow but, fortunately, the city was better prepared for it this time and Father's usual assistance was not required.

How to keep dry in the rain

CHAPTER 17

Jubilee

1978 was Father's fiftieth as an officer of the Glasgow Humane Society, a year that brought many celebrations and much pleasure to us all. New Year's day was spent on the river again. Father received word from Police Control that there was the body of a woman in the River Clyde at Jamaica Bridge. We went there immediately in the Land Rover. The body of the woman was floating face-up in the water, about 12 feet from the quay wall.

I went down the wall with Father paying out the rope and shouting instructions. He told me to make sure I got hold of the woman first time, as she was not long in the water and had not yet sunk. I roped her up as Father instructed, and the body was lifted from the water. The woman seemed to have died from shock rather than from drowning. It is a real shame to think that this woman, for some reason known only to herself, was so unhappy at the thought of seeing a New Year arrive that she decided not to live through it.

On January 11th, at around 3 pm, Father was called to the canal at Port Dundas to search for and recover the body of a man from the ice-covered water. Father said the body had only been in the water for about two or three weeks — someone else who didn't want to see 1978.

On Sunday January 15th at around 12.30 pm Father was called by Police Control and informed that there was the body of a man in Queen's Dock. Father and I went there immediately in a Land Rover and launched the boat where the workmen were filling in the dock with rubble. Having manoeuvred the boat through various booms, we found the body floating about halfway along the north wall. Father tied the body up and had the Support Unit, who were in attendance, lift it up the quay wall. He then climbed the ladder up the quayside and examined the body.

On the way back to the launching place we recovered an oil covered lifebelt from among the debris and took it home to scrape and clean the oil off and put it up on one of the bridges where one was missing.

This was one of many little things that Father always did instinctively, like shutting gates that he saw lying open on the river banks. Father was very pleased at this time to hear that the city was opening more of its swimming pools in the summer, and he wrote to congratulate them, as this helped to keep children away from more dangerous water.

The first congratulations on Father's fiftieth year as Humane Society Officer came on the only annual night-out that Father went to, the Police Headquarters Burns Supper. It was amazing how he looked forward to this yearly feast among friends. This year the chairman said a few words about how much the police had appreciated their association with Father over his 50 years as Humane Society Officer, and it was obvious that these words, together with the standing ovation that he was given, gave Father a lot of pleasure.

One day in March at about 2 pm, father was called by the Information Room to Yorkhill Dock where the body of a man had been seen in the river. Father and I went there immediately. The body was at the foot of the ferry steps, a man of about middle age, 4 to 5 weeks in the water. It was a windy, blustery day and, as Father caught hold of the body it rolled over in the river's swell and a polythene-wrapped package floated out from inside the man's coat. Father shouted for me to catch it before it sank, as papers can often be the only clue to identification.

The body was lifted up the ferry steps and laid out in the 'waiting room', the little hut to keep the wind and rain off passengers while waiting for the ferry. I opened the plastic bag and, to my amazement, found it was money. Two policemen, Father and I laid the notes on the floor of the hut alongside the body, each one with a stone on it to stop it being blown away. In all we laid out £680 in £5 and £10 notes. What a strange scene we must have made. The three of us, the body and all this money neatly laid out. It is highly probable that this man who had lived in a city model (a working man's hostel) and carried his savings with him had been the victim of an attempted mugging. He was probably running along the quay wall clutching his savings to escape from some would-be robber, or actually fighting them off, when he slipped and fell into the water, but we shall never know.

A few days later Father was called to the Clyde at the Kingston Boat Company premises, where there was a man in the water. Father launched his boat at the back of the weir and proceeded downriver. The man's body was found lying on the mud flats that have formed in the river at this point and show at low tide. Father roped the body up and threw the ropes up onto the quay wall. Slowly the body was drawn from the mud and lifted up the wall. Father said that the man had, in his opinion, only been in the water since the previous night.

Going upriver one day in April with a party of city officials who were looking at facilities on the river, we came across a woman's body lying over the 'island' just below Belvidere. This 'island' is formed where there used to be coal mines. Sticking up in the centre of the river is part of a stone wall with earth and trees growing out of it. The north side of this is deep water, the south side is shallow, and full of old dead trees. This body was lying on the south side. Father tied it up and we had quite a difficult time pulling it free from the trees because of the way the body had been washed by floodwater down onto the logs.

The body. which had been in the water for several weeks, was taken back to our wharf. She must have been lying against a tree on her face, as it was marked badly. It was one of the worst faces of a woman that I have seen to date. This incident was bizarre because we had to put the officials who had been with us onto the bank, and there they sat with their flasks of tea and sandwiches as we dealt with the recovery of the body.

On Tuesday, 18th April 1978 I entered the Clyde at Albert Bridge to save a woman. The only way to get her out was for police on the bridge to throw down a rope, which I fastened to her, and they started to pull her to safety. She started shouting that we were breaking her arms. In the circumstances, it was good to hear her shout as the pain would keep her from lapsing into unconsciousness — better a broken arm than dead (as it turned out her arms were uninjured as far as I know). When the police had hauled her up to the parapet they found they couldn't lift her any higher as she was being caught under the bridge. I shouted for them to pull me up alongside her, and while I was suspended in mid-air I managed to move her out from the bridge enough for the police to lift her the rest of the way. I climbed up onto the outside ledge of the bridge and helped lift the woman over the parapet into the waiting arms of the ambulancemen.

While I was in the water, Father was launching his boat at the back of the weir to be on hand if I needed help. It is amazing how fast Father could move in a case like this. I had raced by car, then sprinted to the scene, yet in these few minutes Father had managed to reach the back of the weir by Landrover and trailer, and to launch his lifeboat.

How reassuring it was to know that, if I got into difficulties, expert help was close at hand. Father was really worried about me going to a rescue without a boat, but when he saw me safe and well he was happy and proud. I knew that it had been Father's superb training that had helped me, and I was glad to have followed his example of forgetting about one's own safety when someone is in trouble. I took the spectacular way to the rescue, but it would have been Father in his unassuming way who would have had to rescue us both if anything had gone wrong!

The following Friday April 28th, at about 5.45 pm, I again entered the Clyde near the Albert Bridge, and this time saved a man from drowning . Again Father was doing the 'back-up' in case I got into trouble.

For these rescues I was awarded the Strathclyde Regional medal for bravery and a Bar. Father was very proud of me, but did not attend the presentation ceremony as the River Clyde was in flood again and he wouldn't leave his telephone in case someone got into trouble with the heavy rainfall that had deluged the city, so Mother and Ann accompanied me.

Danger man of the river

HE'S the best-known man on the river. For stocky Ben Parsonage has saved 170 lives.

When the river-watchers see 57-year-old Ben in the stern of a boat on a river or canal around Glasgow it means trouble.

Perhaps a child has toppled from the towpath . . . or perhaps his task is much grimmer.

Ben, who has won three Corporation medals for bravery, is Glasgow Humane Society Officer.

He grew up by the River Clyde. Now he lives with his family in an attractive villa in Glasgow Green and hires out boats on the Clyde.

But business halts whenever Ben gets a call that he is needed on the river.

H

Rescue His Business, The Clyde His Life

On April 12th *The Evening Times* carried this story:

HONOUR FOR BEN.
A man who has saved more than 300 people from drowning is to be honoured next month. He is 75 years old Mr. Ben Parsonage, whose 50 years of heroic work with the Glasgow Humane Society is to be marked with a civic lunch in the City Chambers on June 5th. Yesterday Police Committee Chairman, Nancy Ballantyne said "We all owe him a debt of gratitude. Most people will welcome the news that Mr. Ben Parsonage is to be honoured for his 50 year's service to the city. This gesture is long overdue."

OLD MAN RIVER
After 50 years of faithful services Glasgow honours the king of the Clyde. If you cut old Ben Parsonage, it's doubtful if there would be any blood. The liquid that would flow from his veins would possibly bear an uncanny resemblance to the murky water of the river he loves with an intensity that almost hurts.
To deny that the Clyde is part of the old man of the river, would be to deny that the trees which line its banks need sunshine and rain. It is an affinity that began 75 years ago when young Bennie came into the world a stone's throw from one of the world's most famous rivers in Bridgeton, Glasgow.
And it is a partnership to which more than 300 people and an unknown number of potential suicide victims today owe their lives.
For during 50 years of dedicated, unstinting service to Glasgow Humane Society, Ben has saved all these people from a watery grave.
To understand the gratitude which has promoted the district council, Strathclyde Regional Council, the Chamber of Commerce, banks and city businessmen to plan a civic lunch for him next month and start a fund to honour him, you have to understand the depth of the unswerving devotion the man has for his work. His wife Sarah chuckles as she explains how she met her future husband by the river, married him in the city of Glasgow boathouse and has lived ever since with him within earshot of its lapping waters. To her, the Clyde is like Ben's mistress, but a mistress with whom she has built up a working, compatible relationship over the years. They were married on a Friday, but there was never any question of a honeymoon. The next day the Klaxon in the boatshed sounded and Ben was out in his boat answering yet another call.
But the job has its sad, at times gruesome, side. Over the years many onlookers have seen him step from his boat, tears in his eyes, and carry the dripping body of a drowned child up the bank in his arms.
In his time he has pulled about 2,000 bodies from rivers, canals and streams in an around the Glasgow area. It is an unpleasant, but necessary task, and Ben does it with a skill that constantly astounds the police.
Officers often spend hours dragging the depths of a waterway for victim only to give in and call in old Ben, and invariably, his dragging equipment and his sixth sense will locate the body.

"I have a special feeling", he explains in his wavering voice "I can always tell when I touch a body. It is like a telephone message, flowing up through the irons and the ropes of my equipment to me. It is a strange thing you only get through experience."

"I remember a boy was drowned bathing in a disused quarry. The water was 90 feet deep. Have you any idea what a body feels like at that depth? It is as light as a feather. The police couldn't find it, but I managed to locate it.

He knows every yard of the river and will often stand for hours on end at his window overlooking its shores on Glasgow Green just gazing at it. He has spent days hacking away at trees and undergrowth on the banks to have a clearer view of children playing nearby and be certain of their safety. As he talks, his tiny 5 ft 1 in frame comes alive and his moon face lights up as the memories come flooding back.

He recalls the time he watched a man acting strangely on St Andrew's Suspension Bridge, and approached him to try to talk him out of doing anything stupid.

The man recognised Ben and explained that the old man had pulled him out of the river some years earlier on a previous suicide attempt. He said that this time he planned simply to throw a suitcase of belongings into the Clyde to rid himself of bad memories and then go off and start afresh. The man did, but typical of Ben, he later slipped out in his boat and retrieved the suitcase and handed it in to the police "just in case he changed his mind".

Ben has great difficulty in analysing his strange love for the river, an obsession which began as a lad in short trousers when he used to help his predecessor bail water from the boats.

"I just love the river, and I love boats, and I love rowing. I can't explain it, but I never get fed up with it. And I love to help other people."

"I get a great feeling when I pit myself against the elements. When there is a heavy run on the river, I like to be able to master it, and to row against it"

"It is a great river, a unique river, and it is cleaner now than it has ever been in all the time I have known it. There are ducks on it now, and where there are ducks there must be other forms of life".

"I'll be here as long as they need me. If I am asked to go anywhere, I will go, no matter the time of day or night."

The *Evening Times*, May 1st 1978.

On June 6th the Scotsman was able to report:

LIFESAVER HONOURED

Ben Parsonage was persuaded to leave his beloved River Clyde yesterday for a hero's reception. He was guest of honour at a luncheon in Glasgow's City Chambers. And the man who has witnessed hundreds of tragedies during his 50 years patrolling the river was overcome by the occasion. He said "Words fail me."

During the luncheon many people paid their personal tribute to Father. The Lord Provost, David Hodge said:

"We are gathered here today to honour Ben Parsonage. All of us, I think, could speak at length on Ben and on the Glasgow Humane Society of course, and together they have done so much for Glasgow, the City of Glasgow, for Clydeside, through the years, but at this moment I would not care to say much more than that because with us today we have someone who has known Ben, Ben Parsonage the man, his work, his tradition, all that he has done and all that he is still going to do. As I say there is someone here who is very well able to speak of him and his work, a life-long friend of his, someone who in the high office of Chief Constable was constantly in touch with Ben and the work that he was doing from day to day in the City — so I have very much pleasure indeed on calling on Sir James Robertson to say a word or two regarding our friend Ben Parsonage.

As one who has known and worked with Ben Parsonage for over 25 years and has had many opportunities of assessing the value of his great work, it is a great honour to me to be invited to deliver this speech today.

In any essay on 'Heroes' Thomas Carlyle wrote that he had come to discourse on a great man, his manner of appearance in the City's business, what ideas men formed of him and what he did.

I, too, have undertaken to discourse on a great man — not a great man in stature but one with a great heart – a pocket Hercules, Ben Parsonage. He has demonstrated often these qualities for almost 60 years 50 of these as an Official of the Glasgow Humane Society.

But I am able to tell you only a mere fraction of what he has done for Glasgow. The Glasgow Humane Society was formed in 1790 from money left by Mr James Coulter. In the 188 years since then, that bequest of £200 has made it possible to rescue thousands of people who were attempting to commit suicide or had fallen into the water through accident. Hundreds of children of successive generations have been rescued from a watery grave through the preventive actions of the Humane Society Officer.

In 1790 the population of the City was 70,000 because Gorbals, Calton and Anderston were still separate burghs and not part of the City. There were no paid Police Forces then and certainly no Police Life Savers or Frogmen. The City was policed by the male citizens themselves. So we can appreciate just how important and invaluable would be the rescue work carried out by the Glasgow Humane Society.

I am certain that none of the Humane Society's Officers has served the City and District as long as the present Officer Ben Parsonage, whose first recorded recovery from the water was 1918 — 60 years ago.

He was born from the union of an English father and a Rutherglen girl. He was born in Bridgeton and was much attracted to the nearby river.

Recently, in answer to a question as to why he took up this type of work, Ben

Ben, George and Sarah with a rowing trophy

"She knew she had to compete......."

replied, "I just love the river — and I love boats. I can't explain."
It was just these qualities of manhood which attracted a local girl who began to come about the station. He, too, saw in her many qualities which he admired. These qualities included a pretty face, a delightful disposition and a wholesale respect for the river, the vagaries of which her husband-to-be had to face each day and night. Their romance blossomed. An old song describes the difficulty of courting in a crinoline but, most unusually, this young couple spent their courtship in a rowing boat, being rowed by Ben between the weir and the King's Bridge.
Sadie knew what she was taking on. She knew she had to compete with Ben's affection for the river and his dedication to his dangerous calling but her very nature and upbringing had prepared her for the part she had to play in his life. They were married in the boathouse in 1933. Ben was called out early next morning to recover a boy from the canal. On the day of the marriage some wag displayed a notice on Suicide Bridge — a notice which said:
"Don't jump today, Ben won't be here."
Sadie felt she would always come second in his heart but, having known the family like many of you, for may years and having spent time in the family circle, I can confidently assure her that, despite her early fears, she has triumphed over her rival, the river, and now stands a clear first in Ben's love and affection.
The major contribution of Mrs Parsonage, apart from keeping her husband fit and clear of domestic worries, was in the field of caring for those rescued and acting as comforter and adviser to those whose plight had driven then to the river. Many other Glasgow Green injuries were treated by one or other of the Parsonage family in the Casualty Station. In effect the Glasgow Humane Society was receiving the services of four for the salary of one.

Sir James went on to acknowledge Father's many qualities, to speak of his life at the Green, with Mother and the family. He quoted many sources and told stories of Father's powers. How proud we all felt, listening to his words.

On call,as he is over a 24 hours period, and never having been known to fail to answer the telephone. He would never leave the house with the telephone unattended. Each call for help signified some danger to him, but he never shirked, no matter the state of the wind or the weather.
In addition to being the recipient of the British Empire Medal, the Corporation Medal and two Bars, he has expressions of thanks from many parts — home and abroad — including a tie from a lady whose son he had rescued from drowning. Many of the children rescued in the past are now parents themselves and they certainly don't forget.
I myself while Chief Constable had occasion often to write to Ben in acknowledgement of his bravery and of his help to the Police.
His family and those around him adore him for his sterling qualities and his indomitable courage.

His knowledge of currents and ledges and the action of water on bodies have often enabled him to forecast accurately where a body is likely to come up or be found. His patience and perseverance at recoveries are a great comfort to relatives.

The existing record of what he has done for mankind, although impressive, is but a fraction of the whole history of his work. But, in fairness to this brave man, I feel I must read a selection from many letters from the Police for his help to them in murders, suicides, accidents and in the recovery of articles — criminal and otherwise. One letter reads: 'Your help was given in the usual ungrudging fashion we have come to expect from you, showing infinite determination and patience during 36 hours on the river when turbulence threatened your life.'

A second letter reads: 'Despite appalling weather conditions you continued your search until you recovered the child's body'

On one occasion, boys were trapped on bridge girders. Ben propped a ladder from the boat and climbed on to the girders. With the use of a rope which was thrown to him, he lowered them slowly down 50/60 feet above water, into the boat.

Many nice things have been said about him in the Press, examples of which are: Ben does his beat in a row boat, Ben to the rescue again, Glasgow's river rescue champion.

There are many other directions in which he helped the City, helping the scouts with knots, rescues from flooded houses, help at regattas — rescues of crews, etc.

You and I know little of what prompts people to contemplate suicide and we never appreciate the grim tragedy, danger and sadness which Ben and his family share, and yet 50 years afterwards he is still carrying on courageously. While visiting a country village, a tourist spoke to the oldest inhabitant and asked the old man: "Have you lived all your life here?" "Not yet", replied the old man.

Ben has not lived all his life yet and for the sake of many whom he will continue to rescue, comfort and sustain, thank goodness he is to continue to serve Glasgow Humane Society.

Yes thank goodness that Ben Parsonage, B. E. M., Corporation Medal and two Bars, 'Guardian of the river', 'Glasgow river rescue champion', 'King of river rescues' — whatever title appeals to you, has not yet lived all his life amongst us.

I'm very grateful that we'll have the continued services of Bennie and the Parsonage family in the interests of mankind in this City.

There is in our midst today, and with this I finish, the Rev. John Logie of Oyne in Aberdeenshire, formerly a minister of the Central Church in Charlotte Street. When Mr and Mrs Parsonage were celebrating their 40th Wedding Anniversary he composed a poem — I was asking him would he not read it today. I think he did an excellent job. Five years have passed but it's still appropriate, it's headed

— 'This Is Your Life'
>Way back in nineteen thirty three
>Two young folk said they would agree
>To pledge their troth in wedded life
>And settle down as man and wife
>
>So that same year at Christmas-tide
>They came to live by the river Clyde
>They learned to pull a joint oar
>While children came, first one, then more.
>
>They brought them up with loving care
>And taught them to be just and fair
>No finer family could be seen
>Throughout the whole of Glasgow Green
>
>Of course, they've had their ups and downs
>They've had life's blessings and life's frowns;
>Joys, sorrows, disappointments, pain,
>They've overcome, time and again.
>
>Yes, overcome! Because, above
>All else, they trust the God of love
>Whose strength and comfort, grace and peace
>Have brought a joy that cannot cease
>In thankfulness for forty (now forty-five) years
>Of sharing happiness and tears,
>To gallant husband, gracious lady
>We wish good cheer, dear Ben and Sadie.

Ben and Sarah

Rescue His Business, The Clyde His Life

Again Lord Provost David Hodge rose to his feet:

I think Sir James has given you some idea of why we are here today. It's my very happy task now to hand over something which is by no means the recompense that Ben Parsonage deserves for what he has done. His services are beyond price. There's no question of this. There are many people, so many of your friends and associates who think so highly of you, they have joined together to make this little presentation to you — they've given me the job of handing it over to you. I do this with the greatest possible pleasure and I would ask you to please accept on behalf of all your friends, all those who know you, know your work, know the years of devoted service you have given to us and hopefully you're going to give many more, may I please ask you to accept on behalf of all of us this gift.

Father surprised us all by saying a few words:

"My Lord Provost and friends, I do not think I could express in words my feelings today. I am very proud to share this happy occasion with my wife and family who have helped me so much over the years. I thank everyone concerned for their kindness. I love helping others, it is a wonderful feeling when you rescue someone and great a satisfaction when I recover a body as this brings relief to friends and relatives and is greatly appreciated. I hope I have always carried out the work to the satisfaction of the Glasgow Humane Society and all concerned and shall continue to do so to the best of my ability. I would particularly like to thank my wife for all the help and comfort she has been to me throughout the last 45 years."

The Lord Provost again said a few words:

"The young lady on my left looked at the coffee cups and saucers and saw the Coat of Arms, and the gleam I saw in her eye I felt we were going to end up one short today. She was admiring it, it is rather a nice coat of arms of course and rather nice coffee cups but I thought — well perhaps having the Coat of Arms around her and so on — we'd better send her away content — it might save the cups and saucers — if we gave her something with the Coat of Arms on it.[Then Mother was presented with two small plaques with the Glasgow Coat of Arms]. Now George, I hope you were listening to all that Sir James has said today, you might get a few notes to add to the copious volume which you are preparing — the book which of course will be the Parsonage Story, will be appearing and I'm looking forward very much to reading it — I hope George that you will give me an autographed copy so for heaven's sake go to the night school and learn to read and write. I thank you all most sincerely for coming to pay tribute to this grateful man, he's still with us, just getting geared up now for the next 50 years. I know he'll be with us for a long time and I know he's tremendously active on

232

the Clyde — indeed he's much better in a boat than he is on his feet and I sincerely hope he'll be with us to carry on the wonderful work he has done over the years — to himself and to the family, Glasgow says "Thank you" sincerely. There is still another little duty to be performed today. Our Lord Dean of Guild, Mr Barnes-Graham, has a very pleasant task to perform — something which I think has given a great deal of pleasure to those who know what's happening and I would ask you Lord Dean of Guild, would you please do that now.

The Lord Dean of Guild, Mr Barnes-Graham took the platform next:

My Lord Provost, Lady Provost, Ladies and Gentlemen, especially Ben and Sarah Parsonage, George, Elizabeth and Ann. Much has been said about Ben and I thought Sir James covered the ground most beautifully — because there is so much to be said he could have said too much but he didn't, he gave the beautiful background. We could go on all afternoon and then tomorrow talking of his exploits, for Ben is a legend in his time and his name and his exploits, or some of them, are known to hundreds of thousands of people in Glasgow and the West of Scotland. I, unlike Sir James, haven't known the Parsonage family for long but I knew of him for countless years and it was only when I became ex-officio, a director of the Glasgow Humane Society, I learned the details and I met the man. He is, as he has shown a few minutes ago, a most kindly, a most modest, as well as a most courageous man, and one of the first things that sprang to mind when I got to know him — and more of him was, I thought of the Eamon Andrews Show 'This is your life'. Now I remember vividly a most marvellous life portrayed — Earl Mountbatten — but then when I thought of the footballers and actors, actresses — I thought, my goodness, here is someone who more than qualifies for 'This is Your Life', although he would hate it, he is such a modest man, he would hate to be involved — and that is typical of Ben Parsonage. Now there are a great many people, a great many institutions and bodies, who would be proud and very ready to join the City of Glasgow today in paying honour and respect to Ben. It is quite appropriate that this privilege falls to the Merchant House of Glasgow and my directors and I are most grateful, Lord Provost, to you, to give us this opportunity. The Merchant House, like its sister the Trades House, is now primarily a charitable institution but our past histories go back many centuries and we were very much involved with the development of Glasgow, the development of the Clyde and its facilities. The Clyde which has been the scene, the centre, of Ben's activities for more than 50 years. Ben is a unique personage, I'm sorry for the pun there, but I wonder if it's possible to imagine anyone who is so kindly, so humane, and at the same time so courageous and conscientious in the discharge of his responsibilities over all these years. You might think his conscientiousness and his determination to be available every day in the year, every minute available in case someone was requiring to be saved, was almost carried to be extreme.
Sir James indicated some of this — scarcely ever at church together, perhaps never at church unless communications were intact, nor a bath, until recently

never a holiday, let your mind dwell a little bit along that line and then you will realise the truly conscientious loyalty of the man we are honouring today, and you will realise, as Sir James very rightly drew your attention, something else that Ben could not as a family man, and a very proud family man at that, have continued to maintain such a high standard without the whole-hearted and willing support of his family to so respond. So in honouring Ben, I think we are also honouring Sadie, Elizabeth, Ann and George. In deciding to mark this occasion with a presentation that would be meaningful to Ben and his family, it soon became known to my House that a portrait would be acceptable and accordingly the Merchant House commissioned his son George, not perhaps a well-known portrait painter, but a very well-known visual artist, to paint his father's portrait and I believe this has given great pleasure to Ben and to his family. Now Ben, on behalf of the Merchant House of Glasgow I would like to present this to you from the Merchant's House in appreciation of fifty years gallant service as Officer of the Glasgow Humane Society, along with our very best wishes to you, your wife and family.

These happenings of June 5th 1978 will be in our memories forever.

Tributes

The Ben Parsonage BEM trophy, for the lightweight sculling championship of Scotland presented on his 50th year as Officer of the Glasgow Humane Society 1928-78 by his son George.

The above inscription appears on a rose bowl that I presented to the Rowing Association for its annual competition. I had for many years been Scottish Sculling Champion, and had tried to introduce a lightweight section into rowing, so when the association decided to inaugurate a lightweight championship in the same year as Father's fiftieth year celebrations, it seemed an obvious presentation to make.

I was very pleased to win this cup in its first year

Assistant Chief Constable Petrie of Strathclyde Police paid this tribute to Father on his 50th year as Officer:

I can't remember 'trying property' in Carlton Place on Beat 9A in the old Southern Division of the city of Glasgow Police in March 1946, a brand new 'rookie' straight out of the RAF with a Class B Release. It was the last hour of the night shift and cold and foggy. There was a splashing in the river but no shouts. As I ran over to investigate there was a cheery "Hello" from the diminutive figure in a rowing boat carefully wending his way down stream from the weir on the River Clyde.

That was my first view and meeting with 'Old Man River' himself Ben Parsonage BEM. If you choose the right morning in 1979 you would see the same scene — only 'young' George, his son, would be providing the oar power.

He was on his way to find a body reported in the Clyde in the Marine Division, I learned. But he was proceeding down the *south* bank of the river! It may have been in the Marine yesterday but it would be lying in an unknown pool about 130 yards south of the Govan Ferry steps when Ben Parsonage went to the spot. Absolutely uncanny!

I do not propose to talk on specific cases or requests for assistance to the Glasgow Humane Society which I initiated during a career in the Southern, Northern, Eastern and Maryhill Divisions of Glasgow Police.

My main involvement with 'Bennie' was I think in writing and recording letters of thanks for unbelievable feats of endurance, modes of rescue and deeds of courage performed by this remarkable man during my sojourn in the Chief Constable's Office in St Andrews Street, Glasgow. These will be told in detail by officers personally involved and no doubt by the rescued or their families — and they will read like fiction since they will not be coming from the lips of this modest and dedicated public servant.

It has been my privilege to be associated with the legend that is Ben Parsonage of the Glasgow Humane Society. he has received the recognition of Sir Malcolm McCulloch, Sir James Robertson and Sir David McNee as Chief Constables of Glasgow and of Mr Patrick Hamill, Chief Constable of Strathclyde as well as Lord Provosts of the City of Glasgow on more occasions and for more years than I can recount. He has also received the recognition of Her Majesty The Queen.

My tribute to him therefore pales into insignificance in the face of these public personalities. Suffice to say that it is not often that one meets and shares experiences with the continuing legend of the River Clyde that is Ben Parsonage.

Having started my Police career in Govan with its docks, the River Cart, and the Brock Burn it is obvious that we had to meet from time to time which we did. However, it was when I moved to the Eastern Division — in your home division — and in particular my appointment as Enquiry Sergeant that caused us to be most often in contact — not always for morbid reasons! It was during that period that I first met your family and realised how much they actively involved themselves in your work and of whom you are so rightly proud.

What most impresses me and I am sure all Police Officers who know you — and that must be most of the Glasgow Officers — is your tremendous knowledge of all the waterways in the area and in particular the River Clyde. If the exact point of entry and the time could be given it was uncanny how accurate your area of search became. More than once I have heard you say that the information given must be wrong because the body was not where it should have been and when, after further interrogation, amended information was given you went straight to the spot and made the recovery.

It must give you and your family tremendous satisfaction to know that over the years you have been responsible for saving many persons from drowning. While your efforts could not always save life, your speedy recovery of bodies has been of great benefit to bereaved relatives by removing the uncertainty and strain of hoping when common-sense says there is no hope.

I know you are not yet ready to retire and put your feet up although no one is more entitled to do so. I know that you are and have been for many years ably aided and abetted by George in carrying out your essential tasks, long may you be able to continue. Please give my regards to Mrs Parsonage and your family.

With all good wishes,

Yours very sincerely,

Leslie McLaren

Of course during those times the river work went on as normal. At this time of year Father was always asked to stand by on the river when the parachutists did their annual stunt of landing in the park, just in case the wind took them off course. Fortunately, I can only remember them being blown off course once, and then they landed far away from the river.

Bodies were recovered from the Clyde in the harbour, and at Polmadie, and a man in a tiny dinghy so small for the Clyde that he was a danger to himself, had to be taken from the water.

Saturday July 8th 1978 saw the Orange Walk with all its bands and members and followers on assemble in the Green. Among the thousands of people were one or two who wanted to swim the river, and one who jumped in. A youth started to take his clothes off downstream of the wharf. We rushed down and escorted him from the banks. He was insisting that he was still going to swim so the police removed him for his own safety. A short time later another youth jumped from the suspension bridge into the river. Fortunately we brought him out safely after a race across the river in our lifeboat.

In August another case occurred in which Father's knowledge amazed me. Late one night he received a phone call from the Marine Police that a patient from the Western Infirmary had jumped off the Argyle Street Bridge over the Kelvin. We rushed there. Below where the man had fallen there was sloping bank. The police said that even if the man had hit the bank he would have rolled into the water, after all it was about a 20 to 25 foot fall. Father informed us all, and I certainly had never heard this before, that if you fall from a height onto a sloping bank, the slope breaks your fall, so Father thought that the man would have escaped. This proved to be the case, as the man turned up at his brother's house the following morning.

On September 10th at 1.30 am we were awakened from our sleep by the sound of a klaxon. On rushing to the window we saw a police Range Rover sitting on the road in front of the boats. Father and I pulled some clothes on and rushed out of the door. For some reason we had not been telephoned about Father's help being required at Shettleston Road, where people were trapped by floodwater in a bus.

We raced to the spot and launched the boat. The water was between 6 and 8 feet deep and was swirling, forming small whirlpools over the drains in the road. The single-decker bus contained a wedding party still in their evening dresses and suits.

The women, holding their skirts clear of the water, then the men, were helped into the boat and ferried a few at a time to dry land.

Later that September, Father was informed by telephone that there was a body in the water at West Street. A Land Rover was sent for, but to save time and because of the state of the tide we went downriver in our motor boat and over the ramp on the weir gate.

As we approached the George V Bridge we spotted a tiny rowing boat at the stern of the old fire boat. We hurried towards them to discover that they had rowed their boat over the body and it had then disappeared.

After further questioning, Father came to the conclusion that the body, which they said was that of a woman, had only been in the water for a short time, not sinking until the boat had dislodged the last pockets of air in the woman's clothes. A police Inspector who had been on the Bridge said she had looked like an Asian woman in a sari. Father searched as best he could around the fire boat.

The CID from Craigie Street arrived, as someone had reported that the woman had been thrown in. We managed, with help from the police and workers, to loosen the fire boat and slide it downriver to give Father a clear area for his search. After about 10 minutes he picked up the woman's body. It was lifted onto the quay, where the police doctor examined her, and police photographers took pictures. The body was removed for an immediate post mortem, but it turned out that there were no suspicious circumstances.

On Thursday, October 12th, Father received word from police control that there was a body of a man in the Forth and Clyde Canal at Bishopbriggs, near the Sports Centre. When we arrived at Bishopbriggs we had difficulty in getting along the canal bank because of the high weeds. Launching the boat proved to be even more difficult because of the 10 feet or so of reeds at the water's edge, so we had to wade into the canal to get afloat.

The body had never sunk, and Father had to be careful getting hold of it. It was that of an oldish man; a very, very big man; he must have put up an awful struggle while drowning as his jacket, which was floating nearby, had its sleeves inside out and his coat was entangled round his legs. In his clenched fist he had his false teeth. Father had to hold the body with the ropes he had tied around the shoulders while I rowed along the canal for about one mile to a spot where the coffin shell could attend on the banking. Due to weeds this took about an hour. The casualty doctor and a forensic cameraman attended. A dog, thought to be the dead man's, was found running up and down the bank.

On November 2nd at 9.50 am Father received word that there was the body of a man in the River Clyde at Yorkhill Dock. We proceeded there in the Land Rover, climbed down the ladder on the quay wall, fastened the body up and had it lifted out.

You may have noticed that quite a few cases I have mentioned in the last year involved Father or myself going down the quay wall by a ladder or on a rope to reach the body. That was because there was nowhere to launch a boat on this walkway. It is not as easy as it sounds to climb down the quay wall, oily ladders, freezing fingers whipped raw with the west winds or hanging suspended by a rope, trying to hang onto the rope or ladder with one hand while using the other to tie up a body, or trying to hook a leg around a rung to enable you to use both hands. not easy at all. If you don't believe me, try it sometime! The steps couldn't come soon enough.

Towards the end of the year more tributes were paid to Father's jubilee. The following cutting from the newspapers and the ensuing night out was very much appreciated by Father and Mother.

AWARD FOR LIFE-SAVER BEN

Despite tributes that poured in over the years, Ben Parsonage, the man who must be Glasgow's best known life-saver, had never been formally honoured by the Royal Life Saving Society. That'll be remedied next month, though, when Lord Provost David Hodge, hands over a certificate of thanks from the Society at a ceremony in the City Chambers. *Evening Times* September 19th 1978.

As I said earlier in the story, Father was an active member of the Clydesdale Rowing Club and, in fact, was a Life Member. Clydesdale held one of their 'confined' Regattas and Launchings, after which they always have a tea party upstairs in the clubhouse.

Father and Mother were invited to this Regatta and after the presentation of prizes to the Regatta winners, the club presented Father with a plaque of the Clydesdale badge, suitably engraved for the occasion, on his completion of 50 years as Officer of the Humane Society, and a little girl presented Mother with a beautiful bouquet of flowers. Again, we had a wonderful evening.

The Glasgow Schools' Rowing Club purchased a fine single sculling boat, and it gave all the family great pleasure when the President of the Schools wrote to Father asking permission to name the boat the Ben Parsonage, BEM. The boat was launched by my sister, Ann.

In December 1978 the Glasgow Argonauts decided to hold a Tub Pair race as a tribute from the oarsmen of Glasgow, and indeed Scotland, to Father: 'The Ben Parsonage Regatta'! On a pouring wet day, oarsmen from many parts congregated to race in pairs and 'scratch fours'. Although the weather was bad, a good day's racing was held in Elite, Veteran, and Junior pairs and in Fours. A presentation

Ben and Sarah in later years

of a pocket watch was made to Father on behalf of the oarsmen.

Mother, Father, Ann, Elizabeth, and her husband John, my nephew Bruce, and of course myself, were all at the University Boat Club to hear the nice things that were said, but of course, we were still within hearing distance of our telephone!

The *Evening Times* said:

MEN OF THE CLYDE WILL HONOUR A LEGEND.
The oarsmen of Glasgow will assemble on the Clyde next month — to pay tribute to a man whose humanitarian work on the river is a legend. The get-together will include a presentation to Ben Parsonage. It's not the season for a regatta, but we think it's important to turn out and say thank you to a man who has contributed so much to the good image Glasgow deserves. Basically it's a fun day. At this time of the year you can't expect to break records in rowing.

On December 13th, at about 3.50 pm, a Land Rover arrived at the house door and the crew said they had been sent to take us to the Kingston Bridge area, where Father's help was needed. We hitched the trailer and hurried down to Kingston, the exact locus being received on the police radio, just west of the bridge on the north bank. I went down the ladder with Father holding the ropes, which I fastened up under his supervision. The body was then lifted up the quay wall. It was very badly swollen, and blood was pouring from the eyes. The CID arrived and thought the blood suspicious, but Father said he had seen this happen before, depending on how the body had been lying, and that it was quite natural. Father said that the body had been about six weeks in the water, and, as usual, that proved to be quite accurate and helped the police in the identification.

A few days later, the CID had Father attend at Allan's Pen, as they sought his advice after the discovery of a woman's body on the river bank, where she appeared to have frozen to death.

On January 25th 1979 at about 4 pm Father received a phone call from the Police Information Room, saying that there was a body or at least part of body, in the river near to Shieldhall Wharf. The Motor Vessel *Dalmarnock*, moving downriver, was thought to have brought if to the surface and with the fast flowing tide we would have to be quick to get hold of it.

We rushed to the locus and saw an object floating in the water that could have been a body. Due to the lack of a ramp or steps, the boat was lowered into the water by crane and I went down the quay wall on ropes. Under Father's supervision, a canvas sheet was floated under the torso and it was fastened up and lifted out. It was that of a man, but the arms, legs and head appeared to be sawn off. There was also a slash right down the chest.

I then went back down the quay wall to fasten the boat up to allow the crane to lift it back out onto the trailer. Father and the CID examined the remains. Father said that, due to the dismembering and the fact that the body was dead before it was thrown in, he could not tell how long it had been in the water. He said that the body, in his opinion, had not been cut by a ship's propeller. The torso was put into the boat on the back of the trailer and with a police car escort, was taken to the mortuary. The casualty surgeon arrived while we were still there and confirmed that the dismembering was not accidental.

The *Evening Times* gave headlines to this story:

TORSO IN CLYDE
ONE TINY CLUE TO TORSO
RIVER BODY MAY BE GANG VICTIM
KILLER HUNT AFTER RIVER HORROR

Detectives investigating the gruesome discovery of a torso in the River Clyde today would not rule out the possibility that the victim had been killed during fighting between criminal gangs.

The torso was pulled from the river yesterday. The limbs and head had been hacked off before the corpse had been thrown into the water. There is also to be a conference between scientific experts, senior policeman and Ben Parsonage and his son George who recovered the torso. Police throughout Britain have been alerted. Ben Parsonage and his son were called in by police when an unidentifiable object was seen in the water. Said George. "Our boat was lowered into the water by a shipyard crane. As we got close we saw the torso. It was one of the most horrible sights I have ever seen."

PRANK THEORY IN CLYDE TORSO CASE.

It is to undergo forensic examination in an attempt to establish the man's hair colouring.

Were parts of the man's kidneys removed surgically?

The head, arms and legs of the torso were dissected surgically and part of the kidneys from the body are also believed to have been surgically removed by an expert. The post mortem report on further examination by the forensic experts revealed that the head, arms and legs of the body were expertly sawn off. Hospital mortuaries have been checked but no body has been reported missing. Another theory is that a person due for burial or cremation may have been removed from a coffin and rubble substituted. The body could be a corpse donated to a university for medical research and after decapitation and the limbs had been sawn off thrown into the river as a student prank. A team of detectives are searching all ships arriving and leaving the Clyde. Stolen from a mortuary? A check on undertakers?

On January 26th 1979 Father and I attended a meeting with police doctors and CID chiefs from every division, about the torso found the previous night. Father answered questions from many of these officers and gave his opinion. The discussion went on for well over an hour and a half with Father's brains being picked. Statements were taken from the two of us, and we were finished by about 5.40 pm.

It was quite a strange experience to sit in that room listening to Father explaining the reasons for his conclusions to CID pathologists, X-ray experts, doctors, and casualty surgeons. I was very proud to see how willingly and intently they listened. The facts, and the suggestions of how the limbs and head had been removed from the torso, were incredibly gruesome. Some of the ideas put forward were quite astounding yet possible, and gave me an even greater respect for the CID: they really leave no possibility uncovered.

The weeks passed, January moved into February with a search for a murder weapon, stolen goods found, a woman's body recovered from the Forth and Clyde canal, that of a man from the Clyde at Custom House Quay, a hoax on the Clyde, a man missing from Shettleston, and another boy, a young man from below Jamaica Bridge. Yes into 1979 the legend continued.

The Legend Lives On

Father's 51 years of service on the Clyde ended when he died of a sudden heart attack in the early morning of October 1st 1979, just as we were getting ready to go out on the river.

Early in the afternoon word was quietly conveyed to me that the police were worried about the disappearance of a woman last seen in the area of the upper harbour. Equally quietly I slipped away for a short time and ensured that the woman was not lying anywhere along the water's edge; with sadness but without hesitation I had automatically slipped into Father's shoes.

It was with heavy heart and leaden oars that I continued with the duties he had given his life to. I kept turning to an empty space at my side to ask advice. I would run into the shed to show him something, I still expect to see his unmistakable figure coming down the brae and in the gate. Often I felt so alone, on the long cold winter nights of searching, or in the heat of the moment when a split second decision could mean life or death. But slowly I realised I was *not* alone. He had set me such an example that I had only to think. What would he have done? I could go over and over what I was doing in my mind, and somehow he would provide an answer, and for that I am eternally grateful.

"God has been good, I have spent my life doing what I wished to do, to help people and save lives."

Ben Parsonage

Ben and George recovering body of youth from ice

Tributes

I take this opportunity to formally thank all those who paid tribute in their various personal ways to Father's ability, they are too numerous to list but I would like them to know that their sometimes few words of thanks or praise gave him deep satisfaction and all the reward he wanted.

EXTRACT FROM THE MINUTE OF SPECIAL MEETING OF THE DIRECTORS OF GLASGOW HUMANE SOCIETY ON 6th NOVEMBER 1979
TRIBUTE TO THE LATE BEN PARSONAGE BEM
Mr Barnes-Graham opened the meeting by paying tribute to the memory of the Society's late Officer, Mr Ben Parsonage, BEM.
The Chairman went on to recall Ben's 51 years of loyal service to the Society, and his lifetime of service to the City and to his fellow man. He was a man who had, on countless occasions, demonstrated his exceptional courage and great devotion to duty. Many, many people owed their lives to Mr Parsonage, and thousands of bereaved relatives had cause to be grateful for his efforts. Ben Parsonage, Mrs Sarah Parsonage and the family they had together raised, became a unique organisation working skilfully and loyally together in the cause of others. The Humane Society and the whole community rightly felt honoured to have had a man of whom we could be so proud.
Other directors proceeded to add their own personal appreciation and the meeting stood in silent tribute.

Postscript

I now continue the work of the Glasgow Humane Society. The main change from my Father's day is that I combine my work for the Glasgow Humane Society with my job as an art teacher. Most accidents occur outwith school hours and at nightime, weekends and holidays, and so it was decided that as long as I could cope this would be the way ahead.

Every credit must go to Strathclyde Regional Council's Department of Education for this extremely humane decision.

I teach in an open plan school in reasonable proximity to the river and now I have a pager and a portable telephone for immediate alert. I try to check the nearest section of the river to the Humane Society House every morning before school. What is the point of my arriving as school only to be called out to retrieve a lifebelt or to remove a raft, recover stolen goods or something more serious?

Being a schoolteacher has in many ways put me in the forefront of the teaching of safety, which I combine with my art lessons.

My sister Ann, a Senior Librarian with Glasgow City Libraries, gives talks to schools, guilds, Round Tables and similar organisations.

I find my work different in many ways from my Father's day. Father spent much time 'blowing at the myriads of children who dabbled round the river' (Evening News 30/3/50). In those days you could give a child or an adult a row for climbing a fence and explain that fences were put there to be a safety barrier, to keep people out, not to be climbed. But now a lot of river bank fences are broken and, where they are still standing, adults are encouraged to climb them to go to the waters edge to fish. How can you give a child a row for doing something that adults are doing?

In many ways we find the world too fast to bother with small safety items, I find people now do not like anyone to tell them not to do something even if it's for their own good.

Modern day vandalism, the fact that you cannot just leave items lying unattended, has brought about the erection of safety/security fences round the Glasgow Green Wharf. Whereas in Father's day a life boat could for the most part be left for anyone to use in an emergency, nowadays it has to be secured so that when the 'distress' call is made you are sure that the necessary boat is at the ready. Despite these security precautions, this story appeared in the *Evening Times* of May 23rd 1990:

Sarah with the boat named after her

POLICE OUT TO SINK PIRATES
Beware of pirates—that's the message after a spate of break-ins and theft of
valuable equipment.
George Parsonage of the Humane Society, who runs a rescue craft on the
Clyde, suffered two break-ins in 48 hours between Wednesday and Friday last
week.
The robbers escaped with three outboard motors, valued £4,000, from his berth
in Glasgow Green.
The third motor stolen was bought on Thursday to replace the two stolen on
Wednesday night. George hadn't even time to insure the new model and is now
faced with paying the cost, £1,000, out of his own pocket.
He said today: "These thieves could have lost lives. I need to be able to respond
quickly to emergency calls if someone is in trouble on the Clyde."
"We are a charitable organisation and can barely afford the cost of replacing the
motors."

Bolt cutters are carried as part of the regular equipment. In the days of the
Glasgow Corporation a couple of keys fitted any park lock and one or two keys
fitted any lock in the harbour. Now locks are forever being changed and in an
emergency you do not have the time to wait for a keyholder, or to make a detour.

On entering the Green from McNeill Street after dark you will see floodlighting
around the Humane Society House and Wharf. These lights are to assist safe
movement during the many nightime calls.

This is the age of health and safety, and now police officers who accompany
me, and I myself, wear waterproof suits with built-in buoyancy and attached
lifejackets.

The two motorboats (presented by the Glasgow Parks and Recreation Charity
Club), the rowing boats and the boats that sit on trailers are now painted white
with red and blue reflective tape along the sides, The reason for this was partly
Health and Safety (for easy spotting) but also to identify the rescue boats as other
boats were appearing on the waters. Although for the most part I still use the
rowing boat for rescue work the motor launches have become an increasingly
important part of the 'fleet' used when we have to travel fast downstream and
back before the tide at the weir turns, or upstream on the Clyde as far as Belvidere.
The launch has been used to combat one of the plagues of the 80's: removing
rafts so large and well made that they often need 6 or 8 people to lift them from
the water for disposal.

The motor launches and the boats on trailers mean rapid attendance is
possible over a wide radius. The trailers have not changed much, but a jockey
wheel has been fitted to each which enable them to be manoeuvred more easily
into places where a vehicle cannot manage, as happens frequently on river
bankings, or on the occasions when a vehicle is not immediately available for an
accident in the harbour area, when the trailer can be simply run down to the weir
and launched.

DISGRACEFUL
MISCHIEF.

THE Directors of the GLASGOW HUMANE SOCIETY have, at considerable expense, fitted up EIGHT LIFE BUOYS with Ropes, and placed them at various dangerous points on the River, for the purpose of assisting in saving human life. They regret to say that parties have been found so foolish or so wicked as to cut and destroy Four of these Buoys within the last few weeks.

The Directors would appeal to the better feelings of their fellow-citizens to protect this useful apparatus, and if in any case they should witness attempts to injure these means provided for the preservation of valuable life, that they will use every effort to detain and hand over to the Police the perpetrators of such wanton wickedness.

LIFEBELT VANDALS WHO COST LIVES

By PAT ROLLER

A Lifebelt should be just what its name implies—a means of saving life.

But yesterday I discovered that the vandals who haunt the banks and bridges of the Clyde are using them as playthings. When I called on Mr. Ben Parsonage at his home on Glasgow Green, he showed me slashed broken lifebelts he had found floating in the river.

It took only a fortnight to collect his pile.

He said: "I don't know how people can be so senseless.

"Only a few months ago two young chaps dived from the Albert Bridge to rescue an old man.

"They were unable to save him, and it was only thanks to a lifebelt they were clinging to that I was able to rescue them by boat. They were both exhausted."

When I asked the city engineer's department about the vandalism, I was told:

"It's been going on for years but has become more serious lately.

"Several times a week we send a man to inspect every lifebelt—about 30 altogether.

"On almost every visit some of the belts have vanished, or are left slashed and broken. We have replaced as many as nine in a week."

Tragedy

On Thursday a passerby tried to throw a lifebelt form the Albert Bridge to a man struggling in the water.

But the rope holding it to its post was knotted and he couldn't free it.

He ran to a police box, but found the door of the emergency call box rusted and he couldn't open it.

By the time the police were contacted from a telephone box, the man in the water had disappeared.

Yesterday his body was recovered by Mr. Parsonage.

249

When Father was searching in the harbour area and the search was to be continued the next day he tied up his boat alongside a ship and left it safely, now there are no ships and the boat has to be brought home on the trailer every outing.

One thing that doesn't really change is the vandalism of lifebelts. I say 'doesn't really change' because due to improved manufacture they are now practically indestructible!

Over 100 years ago the Humane Society had the notice on page 248 posted.

Over 20 years ago the *Daily Record* carried the story on page 249.

I still remove between 150 and 200 lifebelts from the water every year.

Father used to say that he could put the kettle on for the annual event of flooding during the month of September at various locations throughout the city, especially Shettleston. He would be delighted that I am not now needed for this annual outing to Rigby Street as, by courtesy of Strathclyde Regional Council Department of Sewerage this flooding is now part of history (Bearsden apart).

There are more people on and around the river now, more people own their own racing boat, more people own cabin cruisers, canoeists have arrived on the river, fishermen on its banks, and at times I find it a frustrating job advising on how to use our wonderful river, with its peculiar dangers, in safety. People do not realise the depth of the Clyde (at Glasgow Green we have a depth of 25-30 feet and at the foot of the Belvidere strait 45 feet—more than twice the depth of the Thames at Putney in the heart of London) nor the volume of water that flows down.

In May 1986 Mother received a certificate and a plaque from Strathclyde Police for 53 years service to the Glasgow Humane Society and to the police. It was nice to see the mostly unsung heroine receiving a very just acknowledgement of her services.

For 9 years after Father died, I had my Mother as well as my sister Ann to give me assistance and moral support. As she did with my Father, Mother played a valuable part in the background. With me she had an extra special part to play in that when I was uncertain of what action to take in a difficult situation, she would tell me what Father would have done. She was a marvellous example to us all and when she died after a long and painful illness (19 years in a wheelchair suffering from multiple sclerosis) I felt very alone not only because of the death of my Mother but because I had lost the one tangible remaining link with my Father's knowledge. Fortunately Father had taught me well.

More than 200 persons have been rescued by the present Glasgow Humane Society Officer, many accidents prevented and a much needed and often appreciated service covering many aspects of waterway work is given to the public in Glasgow and the surrounding areas.

And what of the future?

I will continue, God willing, ably supported by my sister Ann. And then, well I go on the assumption that somewhere out there is another George Geddes or

Bennie Parsonage, and I go on teaching and encouraging , hopefully by example, and always on the lookout for the *next* Glasgow Humane Society Officer.

George, Sarah, Ann, Elizabeth and husband John

251

George and Ann in boat